The Wisdom Collection
Quotes and Commentary to Cultivate Self-Knowledge

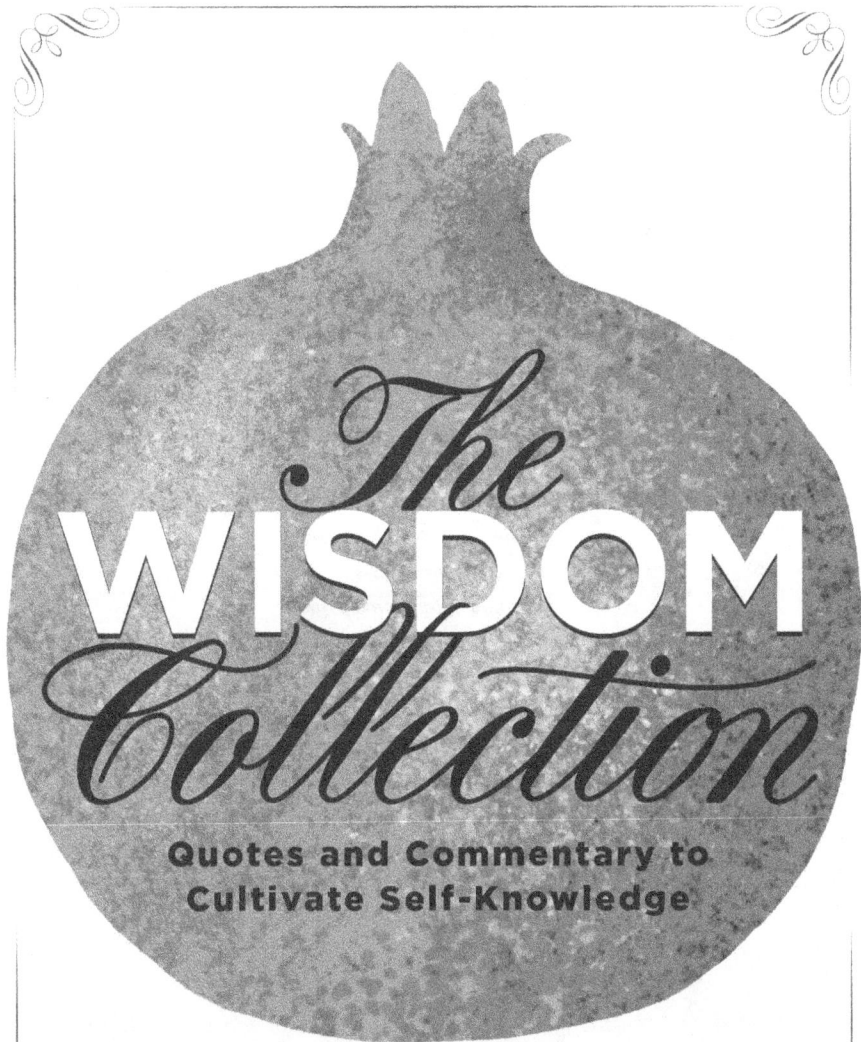

The WISDOM Collection

Quotes and Commentary to Cultivate Self-Knowledge

LISSA COFFEY

FOREWORD BY
CHRISTOPHER KEY CHAPPLE

Bamboo Entertainment, Inc

The Wisdom Collection: Quotes and Commentary to Cultivate Self-Knowledge

Copyright c 2015 Lissa Coffey
Cover art c 2016 Ray Mawst
Published by
Bamboo Entertainment, Inc.
4607 Lakeview Canyon Road Suite 181
Westlake Village, CA 91361

ISBN: 978-1883212278

To all those who teach, who love,
who serve, who nourish our souls...
thank you.

Table of Contents

Foreword

Spiritual Friendship

My best friend lived by quotations. His name was Kenneth Ketwig, and perhaps due to his alliterative name, he lived in a world of sound, of consonance, of words and word smithing. I cheered him on at the regional spelling bee and rejoiced as he advanced to status of National Merit Finalist. We watched Alan Ginsburg on afternoon talk shows and he brought me to Zen and zazen practice and to the Rochester Quakers where I met my wife more than 45 years ago. We read Tolkien in tandem, the Hobbit and The Lord of the Rings. We marched with Cesar Chavez and campaigned for Gene McCarthy. We were there for the first national tours of Ravi Shankar, Janis Joplin, Joni Mitchell, Jimi Hendrix, and the Doors. We performed in plays together, missing Woodstock because of our roles in Aesop's Falables, where he played a grasshopper and I played a tortoise. But most of all he brought me to wisdom, or at least to the possibility of wisdom.

Kenneth always soared while I plodded. Kenneth gathered insight while I followed along. I reveled in and marveled at his letters from Japan when he was a high school exchange student while I stayed home, cleaning offices and painting dormitory rooms.

Kenneth went west to Bellingham, Washington, after high school while I stayed back in New York, eventually moving downstate for university and spiritual training. He later joined us there, settling in Greenwich Village while my wife and I practiced Yoga on Long Island. In the 80s he followed us to California. He settled in San Francisco, where he had mobility, having never learned to drive. His originality and unquenched thirst for meaning brought him to good work as a writer and as a fund raiser for Audubon Society, striving to save the Ballona Wetlands and the California Condor from afar, and eventually as a volunteer development officer for Shanti Hospice.

Kenneth succumbed to AIDS in 1991. His mother rallied young neighbors in her adoptive South Carolina to craft a memorial quilt in his honor. It proclaims, in his own words, his philosophy of life: "Work for Love, Joy and Freedom."

The greatest gift of life is to have a spiritual friend, a friend whose presence reminds us that there is always something greater. There is always more to be found and made. This book is like that special friend.

Savor this book. Approach it thematically. Lissa Coffey has grouped wisdom under topics alphabetically arranged. Approach it at random. Every page exudes wisdom. But most of all, take this book to heart. Let its words bring you to a place of sacred recognition, a remembrance of the sacred silent space at the core of your being. Spiritual practice, as Coffey reminds us again and again, calls us to our center, often in ways delightfully unexpected. Let these apothegms, these sutras, these special words become touchstones for the life well lived!

Christopher Key Chapple,
Doshi Professor of Indic and Comparative Theology,
Loyola Marymount University

Introduction

Wisdom News is a free message that comes out Monday through Friday. I started writing and sending out the Wisdom News newsletter via e-mail in 2001. The format is simple. Each week we have a theme, or a topic. I find quotes about the topic from people, wisdom teachers, throughout the world, and throughout history, and then I provide ideas for ways that we can use this wisdom in our lives right now. Sometimes it's just a different way of looking at things, or something more to think about. It is always fascinating to me that the lessons that people were teaching and learning way back when, are the same lessons that we are learning about today! Some things don't change. The world seems to change all around us, but love is still love, faith is still faith, and wisdom is still wisdom.

This book is a collection of all of the all the quotes and messages that have gone out over the years. We've arranged the topics alphabetically, so that you can read whichever topics appeal to you at the time. You may choose a topic and read a different quote each day of the week, or randomly flip to a page to come across a daily quote meant just for you and whatever particular situation you are in at the moment. You can also sign up for Wisdom News at my website CoffeyTalk.com to get free messages in your e-mailbox on weekdays. And because we have sophisticated technology these days, we also have an APP so that you can carry around this wisdom with you wherever you go.

These quotes may be short, but they are packed with big wisdom. They're like bite-sized pieces that are so satisfying that we want to savor them, and take time to digest them. Each time you read them you'll find that you understand a little more, a little deeper. They could be used as taking off points for topics of discussion with your friends and family, so that you can learn from each other's wisdom and points of view. They could be used in the practice of contemplation, and meditation.

The pomegranate is an ancient symbol found in many cultures throughout the world. Recently it made its way into popularity, not just for its healthy antioxidant properties, but also for its beauty and history. I chose the pomegranate to grace the cover of The Wisdom Collection because it represents knowledge, learning, and wisdom. The pomegranate is bursting full of seeds. Each seed holds the potential for another plant, for more fruit, for many more seeds.

This is how wisdom works. It plants seeds that grow and flourish and feed and nourish our souls. This book is like that fully ripe pomegranate, ready to be opened and enjoyed, with each quote a seed of wisdom to be savored.

Please write in this book, take notes, add your own thoughts and ideas, and share the wisdom with others. It's one thing to read the wisdom, another to understand it, and yet another to live it. The goal is to live it, to embody what we learn and see the truth of who we really are. This self-knowledge is the ultimate goal of life.

Thank you, readers and subscribers, for your wisdom. One by one we are learning and growing and helping to make the world a better and brighter place! *-Lissa Coffey*

CoffeyTalk.com
FaceBook.com/LissaCoffeyTalk
YouTube.com/coffeytalk
Instagram.com/lissacoffey
Twitter.com/coffeytalk
Wisdom Quote Collection for the iPhone in the APP Store

Ability

"He can fit his sails to every wind."
-John Clarke (1596-1658)

Being flexible is an ability we all have, but do we all use it? Have we developed the tools and the skills that it takes to get through whatever comes our way? I don't think we give ourselves enough credit. We might think that we are not capable, not ready, not "enough of whatever" to do what needs to be done. But look at how our abilities shine forth when we need them. Look at how we rise to the occasion when we are called upon. We are strong and we are able. *-Lissa Coffey*

"The winds and the waves are always on the side of the ablest navigators."
-Edward Gibbon (1737-1794)

We are blessed with so much ability. And we can choose to better ourselves and our skills all the time. We might struggle as we learn new things, but as we develop our abilities, these things become easier for us. Have you ever noticed how people who are the best at what they do make even the most difficult of tasks look easy? Olympian ice skaters were not born knowing how to do a "triple toe loop" or some of those fancy moves! But through dedication and perseverance, they are able to master the ice and gravity that plunked them down so many times before. *-Lissa Coffey*

"The workman is known by his work."
-La Fontaine (1621-1695)

This applies in every area of our lives. The artist is known by his (or her) art. Whether the art is music or baking, whether the work is teaching or construction or stock trading - our work is a representation, an expression of ourselves. It's one way that the world recognizes us. It is one way that we contribute to the world. So we must always strive to work to the best of our ability, to do the best that we can do. In doing so we honor ourselves and our abilities. *-Lissa Coffey*

"In the first grade, I already know the pattern of my life. I didn't know the living of it, but I knew the line... From the first day in school until the day I graduated, everyone gave me one hundred plus in art. Well, where do you go in life? You go to the place where you got one hundred plus."
-Louise Nevelson, 1976

What usually happens, is that we are really good at doing what we love to do - so we do it more often and become even better at it! Maybe we love doing it because we're good at it, or the other way around, but it doesn't matter. The idea is to find our "thing," whatever that happens to be, and do it! *-Lissa Coffey*

"There is only one proof of ability: action."
-Marie von Ebner-Eschenbach, 1893

There are all kinds of sayings about this - "Talk is cheap." "Actions speak louder than words." "Just do it." "The proof is in the pudding." We get it! But it doesn't hurt to be reminded of it every once in awhile... To get good at something, to develop our abilities, we need to take action. And we can do that right now, right here. There's no reason to put it off any longer. What are we waiting for? *-Lissa Coffey*

Action

"The only way for evil to triumph is for good men to do nothing."
-Edmund Burke

"This quote reflects Buddhism's teaching on karma, that the future is determined by actions in the present; there is no independent origination. Non-action provides an opportunity for evil to fill the void; thus action is necessary. When we choose the action to take we automatically create our future. This is true of nations as well as of individuals."
-Glenn Hughes, Founder of WISE

There are teachers in our scriptures, our history books, and right in our own neighborhoods... Thank you, Glenn! :-) *-Lissa Coffey*

"We must not, in trying to think about how we can make a big difference, ignore the small daily differences we can make which, over time, add up to big differences that we often cannot foresee."
-Marion Wright Edelman.

Because we are all One, we are all connected, whatever we do, whatever action we take, affects all of us on some level. Our actions are far-reaching. Like the pebble thrown into the pond, the ripples are sent out way beyond the little "splash." There's a bumper sticker that says: "Think Globally, Act Locally." Actions we take at home, right where we are, make a difference everywhere. *-Lissa Coffey*

"Live truth instead of professing it."
-Elbert Hubbard

Actions speak louder than words. We can say something a million times, but when we actually take action, it becomes the truth. It does no good to say one thing and do another. What is a person who's watching you going to believe? Walk your talk. *-Lissa Coffey*

"The world can only be grasped by action, not by contemplation. The hand is more important than the eye... The hand is the cutting edge of the mind."
-Jacob Bronowski, The Ascent of Man

Whenever anything happens, it starts with a thought. But if we JUST THINK about it, nothing happens. Thought followed by action leads to accomplishment, fulfillment, achievement. So, see it, visualize it, declare it to be so, yes! And then take action, take the steps necessary for the thing to be done. *-Lissa Coffey*

"Action is the antidote to despair."
-Joan Baez

Feeling a little blue? Do something! Get out there and take action. There is always plenty to keep us occupied, especially if we have the attitude of "how can I help?" Sometimes we need to just get outside of ourselves to see how we fit into the big picture. By taking action and helping others, we are really healing ourselves, and we are helping the whole world. *-Lissa Coffey*

Age

"You stay young as long as you can learn, acquire new habits and suffer contradiction."
-Marie von Ebner-Eschenbach, Aphorisms (1893)

Learn and grow. This is our theme with WisdomNews. We are here to learn and to grow. That is our purpose. And by doing so, we are becoming better people, and making the world a better place. There's a saying "you can't teach an old dog new tricks." Maybe it's more like "the old dog will learn the tricks he wants to learn." Whatever we want to learn, we can learn that. Our choice. *-Lissa Coffey*

"Age doesn't protect you from love. But love, to some extent, protects you from age."
-Jeanne Moreau, in John Robert Columbo,
Popcorn in Paradise (1979)

Ah, love! There's nothing like it. Love keeps us young. Love is healing. Love is powerful medicine. But where does all this love come from? It's right there inside of us, all the time. We can live a life in love. We can choose love every moment, we can express love, we can give love. -*Lissa Coffey*

**"I never feel age. If you have creative work,
you don't have age or time."**
-Louise Nevelson (1980)

In the spirit world, there is no time, so there is no age. When we lose our awareness of time, then we feel no age. We feel no burdens. We need to spend more time doing those things that make us so happy that we lost track of time. Creative work gives a lot of us that very feeling. -*Lissa Coffey*

**"The fact was I didn't want to look my age, but I didn't
want to act the age I wanted to look either. I also wanted
to grow old enough to understand that sentence."**
-Erma Bombeck, 1979

Erma Bombeck always had such a humorous way of looking at things. This kept her young at heart. She could laugh at life, and laugh at the quirks of our own humanity. Face it, people are funny! Is there any other species that goes to the lengths that we do to maintain our youth? -*Lissa Coffey*

"Years do not always make age."
-George Sand, The Haunted Pool (1851)

What is age, really? A state of mind? Years make up our chronological age – but haven't we all seen people who seem to defy time and look much younger than they actually are? And for some, the opposite is true, too. Age is just a number. Our biological age, mental age, emotional age, and chronological age may all be different numbers. -*Lissa Coffey*

Ambition

**"The significance of a man is not in what he attains but rather
in what he longs to attain."**
-Kahlil Gibran

We can learn a lot about ourselves by looking at our goals and our desires. There's a reason why we want what we want. And we wouldn't want it if it weren't attainable. We learn and grow on the way to our goals. -*Lissa Coffey*

**"Once you say you're going to settle for second, that's what
happens to you in life, I find."**
-John F. Kennedy

Whatever we put out there comes back to us. What we give, we get The energy we create is the energy that we use to propel us forward. When we strive for the best, that's where we go." *-Lissa Coffey*

"The most absurd and reckless aspirations have sometimes led to extraordinary success."
-Vauvenargues

When the Wright Brothers were building their flying machine in the backyard, you can bet that some of the neighbors were calling them crazy. Good thing that didn't stop them! But when we dream big, that's when big things happen – because we make them happen! There are no limitations, so why limit our ambitions? *-Lissa Coffey*

"We can always redeem the man who aspires and strives."
-Goethe

We do what we want to do. When we want to achieve, we achieve. When we want to change, and learn and grow, then we take the steps we need to take to do just that. It starts with a thought, with a decision. *-Lissa Coffey*

"Do not wish to be anything but what you are, and try to be that perfectly."
-St. Francis de Sales

What you are is peace, love, truth, creativity, joy – and so much more. Why would you wish to be anything else, or anything less? Be what you are, be who you are, and together we will light up the world. *-Lissa Coffey*

Angels

"Angels are pure thoughts from God, winged with Truth and Love."
-Mary Baker Eddy, 1875

There are so many different definitions for angels, that we can't really argue "if" they exist or not – angels in some shape or form or thought have a place in this world. We have stories about them, movies and TV shows about them, they are prevalent whether they are on top of a Christmas tree or in a fresco painting. And they are always good and sweet and beautiful. What can we take from this? That there is a loving presence among us! *-Lissa Coffey*

"Angels come in all sizes and shapes and colors, visible and invisible to the physical eye. But always you are changed from having seen one."
-Sophy Burnham, 1990

I think we've all seen an angel at some point in time. My mailman is an angel when he gets out in the pouring rain to deliver a package rather than leaving a note in my box for me to pick it up at the post office. My son's teacher is an angel when she stays after school to tutor her students before a big biology test. My cat is an angel when she curls up on my lap just when I need a hug. We need to recognize the angels in our lives, and appreciate how they can change us just by being who they are. *-Lissa Coffey*

"Sometimes a man, In serving God, Can only do as angels do, and wing it."
-Garry Trudeau

This is our task every day. We don't know what is coming our way, and we can't predict how we are going to handle it. We just "wing it" and do the best we can. We can help each other, we can reach out and give of ourselves – we can be angels. *-Lissa Coffey*

"Angels can fly because they take themselves lightly."
-G.K. Chesterton (1874-1936)

Doesn't this make you smile? Enlightenment means lightening up – so angels are a good example for us! We can laugh, and play, and see the goodness and beauty in life – and not take ourselves too seriously! *-Lissa Coffey*

"I am a little world made cunningly of elements and an angelic sprite."
-John Donne (1572-1631)

This "angelic sprite" is the element that animates us – it's that certain something that gives us our personality, our quirks, our loving spirits. We are not just a bundle of cells, of hydrogen and oxygen and glucose and whatever – we have the capacity to learn and grow and help and heal and contribute. We are made this way by design, so we need to recognize these gifts and use them! *-Lissa Coffey*

Animals

"Animals are such agreeable friends -- they ask no questions, they pass no criticisms."
-George Eliot, 1857

The animals we are most familiar with are our pets. At some point in our lives, I'm sure we've all had at least one pet. I certainly have had quite a few, and I learned something from each and every one of them. Suki is the cat who lives with us right now. I can't really call her "mine" because she is very much her own cat! There is an unconditional love that happens between pets and companions; it's very comforting. If only we could all be such agreeable friends. *-Lissa Coffey*

> "We humans should never forget our capacity to connect
> with the collective spirit of animals. Their energy is
> essential to our future growth."
> -Shirley MacLaine, 1985

Whether or not we have pets, or an affinity for animals, we need to show them our respect and appreciation. We are all in this together – "all" meaning every living creature on this planet. It troubles me that some of our beautiful animals are being so badly mistreated. We have a responsibility to allow animals their space in this world, and to not interfere to the point of causing pain and even extinction. *-Lissa Coffey*

> "Some animals, like some men, leave a trail of glory
> behind them. They give their spirit to the place where
> they have lived, and remain forever a part of the rocks
> and streams and the wind and sky."
> -Marguerite Henry, 1953

My favorite movie in 2003 was "Seabiscuit." The horse was as much a character in that movie as the people that his human co-stars portrayed. You could feel Seabiscuit's love and determination shine. He faced hard times, and overcame tragedy, and contributed so much to the people who came into his life. It's an amazing story, and one that shows the important lessons we can learn from animals. *-Lissa Coffey*

> "The eternal being..., as it lives in us, also lives in
> every animal."
> -Arthur Shopenhauer (1788-1860)

That light shines. If you've ever looked into the eyes of an animal you can see it. It's beautiful, and intense. It's pure, natural, unjaded and precious. Animals are a blessing, a true gift, and we need to recognize this and treat them as such. *-Lissa Coffey*

> "The behavior of men to the lower animals, and their
> behavior to each other, bear a constant relationship."
> -Herbert Spencer (1820-1903)

This is sure something to think about. Maybe when we learn to respect and appreciate other animals, we can more readily respect and appreciate our fellow human being. Maybe it's as simple as following the Golden Rule when it comes to animals – to treat them as we would want to be treated if the hierarchy were reversed. Maybe then we wouldn't have "Mad Cow" disease, or furs as a status symbol, or hunting for sport. *-Lissa Coffey*

Appreciation

"We are told that people stay in love because of chemistry,
or because they remain intrigued with each other, because
of many kindnesses, because of luck. But part of it has got
to be forgiveness and gratefulness."
-Ellen Goodman

If there is any one factor that sustains a relationship it has to be appreciation. Recognizing, and acknowledging, a person's presence in our lives, and the value that they add to the quality of our lives is key. We all have a desire to be appreciated, not just for what we do, but for who we are. And we feel closest to the people in our lives who allow us to feel appreciated. *-Lissa Coffey*

"Much misconstruction and bitterness are spared to
him who thinks naturally upon what he owes to others,
rather than on what he ought to expect from them."
-Elizabeth De Meulan Guizot

Our expectations can get us into trouble, they can keep us from fully participating. Instead of holding back, and asking "what's in it for me?" we can choose to jump in and say: "how can I help?" Instantly, our perspective shifts, and our mood along with it. *-Lissa Coffey*

"Silent gratitude isn't much use to anyone."
-Gladys Browyn Stern

We know that it is good manners to write thank you notes, and yet it always seems to be a chore. Instead, focus on how the person receiving the note feels to receive your gratitude. It's not enough to appreciate someone; we need to express it. We need to declare it, and shout it out sometimes! *-Lissa Coffey*

"When something does not insist on being noticed,
when we aren't grabbed by the collar or struck on the
skull by a presence or an event, we take for granted
the very things that most deserve our gratitude."
-Cynthia Ozick

We wake up in the morning – old hat, think nothing of it. We might even grumble at the early hour, or the cold floor, or the rain. But what a miracle that we have another day at hand! We have another opportunity filled experience to embrace. Where is our gratitude? Start the day with gratitude, and feel that gratitude lift us above any seemingly annoying little non-issues to appreciate all that we have, and all that we are. *-Lissa Coffey*

"I make the most If all that comes and the least of all that goes."
-Sara Teasdale

There's an old saying: "Don't sweat the small stuff." It goes. Let it go. Rather than focus on it and invite it to hang around, instead turn your attention to something that deserves your appreciation. Ah! Doesn't that feel better already? *-Lissa Coffey*

Art

"Art has something to do with the achievement of stillness in the midst of chaos. A stillness which characterizes prayer, too, and the eye of the storm... an arrest of attention in the midst of distraction."
-Saul Bellow (1915 - 2005)

Art causes us to think - it makes us take pause and notice. Ah! In this fast-paced society, it takes a lot to capture our attention. And yet, with some works of art, whether it is a film or a sculpture or a painting, we become immersed in it. What a gift this is, to be able to tune out the chaos and tune in to spirit even for a brief period of time. *-Lissa Coffey*

"There is not a single true work of art that has not in the end added to the inner freedom of each person who has known and loved it."
-Albert Camus (1913-1960)

The beauty of creativity is that is teaches us about ourselves. We are, by nature, creative beings, and when we express our creativity we feel free, we feel boundless - and that is what we truly are. *-Lissa Coffey*

"Life has been your art. You have set yourself to music. Your days are your sonnets."
-Oscar Wilde (1854- 1900)

Every day, our creativity guides us. We are each an artist, and life is our canvas. Life is our instrument, our marble slab, our blank page. All the choices before us are the colors, the notes, the words. We are creating our life as we create a work of art. Let's make it beautiful! *-Lissa Coffey*

"Art attracts us only by what it reveals of our most secret self."
-Jean-Luc Godard

It seems that certain pieces of art "speak" to us. Somehow we can relate to them. Maybe we see something beyond even what the artist intended. It shows how we are all connected. Amazing, how something static can tug on our emotions, touch us somewhere we thought was unreachable. Maybe that's the whole purpose of art. *-Lissa Coffey*

> **"The timelessness of art is its capacity to represent
> the transformation of endless becoming into being."**
> -Lewis Mumford (1895 - 1958)

A piece of art is like this frozen moment of time. It is something that, once complete, doesn't change. It exists just as it is, perfect the way it is. People, on the other hand, are continual works-in-progress. Time doesn't stand still for us. We never seem to be quite satisfied that we are suitable for framing! -*Lissa Coffey*

Authenticity

> **"Somehow we learn who we really are and then live
> with that decision."**
> -Eleanor Roosevelt

Who are you? Or maybe the question is, "who have you decided to be?" We all have roles to play, but our true self is so much greater than any of them. We can identify with the role, or we can choose to see ourselves as the role-player. Our roles come and go and change and grow – and our true self proceeds along through all of it. We can play any role we want to play, do anything we want to do. When we know who we really are, all of this comes easily to us, and we can keep it in perspective. -*Lissa Coffey*

> **"To be nobody-but-yourself – in a world which is doing
> its best, night and day, to make you everybody else
> – means to fight the hardest battle which any human
> being can fight; and never stop fighting."**
> -E.E. Cummings

When you think about all the advertisements and magazines and commercials that encourage us to buy and be made-over and to do this and that to improve ourselves, it's a wonder there's any individuality left at all! We tend to want this actor's hairstyle and that model's figure – or that politician's power and this athlete's paycheck. All of these "things" are held up to us as the ideal. And yet, we know, deep inside, that what is REAL is so much more than that. Though we're inundated by the mega-media machine, we must keep reminding ourselves that what we have to hold onto is who we are, and that is invaluable. -*Lissa Coffey*

> **"The highest courage is to dare to appear to be what one is."**
> -John Lancaster Spalding

The key word here is "appear." So many times it's just easier to put on a mask, to play a role, to go along with what is expected of us. But the courage is in being authentic, in being true to ourselves and our convictions. Being true to ourselves is one thing – but showing the world who we are is another. Do we dare risk judgement? When we are authentic we answer to ourselves, we know that to appear to be anything other, anything less than "what one is" is heart-breaking. -*Lissa Coffey*

"This above all: to thine own self be true."
-William Shakespeare

I love the word authentic. Authentic means genuine, real, true – and when applied to people it means being true to yourself, being your TRUE self, expressing yourself, and nothing less. We sense when people are authentic, just as we can tell when they are imitating, or role playing. When we are authentic, our light shines through, and our path is illuminated. "This above all..." Shakespeare says. It is important to be authentic, important for our well-being and for our spiritual growth. *-Lissa Coffey*

"Any path is only a path, and there is no affront, to oneself or to others, in dropping it if that is what your heart tells you."
-Carlos Castaneda

It's okay to change directions. People have been reinventing themselves since time began. This is a good thing! When our heart leads us somewhere, it's always for a reason. We need to follow and find out what that reason is. Usually this change brings us closer to who we really are, it allows us to discover our true self, and to be more authentic. *-Lissa Coffey*

Awareness

"I break up through the skin of awareness a thousand times a day, as dolphins burst through seas, and dive again, and rise, and dive."
-Annie Dillard, An American Childhood (1987)

How many of our waking hours do we spend actually "aware?" This is a beautiful analogy, I can just picture the dolphins playing, experiencing the freedom and joy that is theirs with every magnificent dive into the beautiful ocean. That same joy is ours, as well. We just need to break up through that skin of awareness and experience it! *-Lissa Coffey*

"Sometimes I think we're all tightrope walkers suspended on a wire two thousand feet in the air, and so long as we never look down we're okay, but some of us lose momentum and look down for a second and are never quite the same again: we know."
-Dorothy Gilman, The Tightrope Walker, 1979

We are always growing and evolving, and we can never go back to where we were once we've grown past it. We've glimpsed the realm of spirit, we know the peace and joy in our hearts, and we want more of it, every day. It is ours! To experience, and to express... be aware of this wondrous gift! *-Lissa Coffey*

"Eden is that old-fashioned House
We dwell in every day
Without suspecting our abode
Until we drive away."
-Emily Dickinson

It's kind of like that song that goes: "You don't know what you've got 'til it's gone…" Know what you've got – you've got SO much!!! We have everything, all of nature, all of creation, all of the infinite possibilities for our lives. And we've got it right here, and right now – open up your awareness to it, accept it, embrace it! *-Lissa Coffey*

"Every dog has its day, but it's not every dog that
knows when he's having it."
-Winifred Gordon, A Book of Days (1910)

Is today your day? Sure it is! Why wouldn't it be? Expand your awareness to include all the beauty and joy and love and peace and goodness that is in you and through you and all around you. Today and every day is your day – recognize it, and enjoy it! *-Lissa Coffey*

"It's exhilarating to be alive in a time of awakening
consciousness; it can also be confusing, disorienting,
and painful."
-Adrienne Rich

Our spiritual pursuits open up our awareness to everything – and sometimes that can be difficult when emotions come to the surface, and stress bubbles up and away. When we know that this is all temporary, and a part of the process, we can observe its happening without allowing it to get us caught up in the drama of it all. We can focus on the big picture – we can see what is truly important, truly real. It is exhilarating, and liberating! *-Lissa Coffey*

Beauty

"Beauty is life when life unveils her holy face."
-Kahlil Gibran

When does life unveil her holy face? When we remove the veil of illusion before our eyes. We see things so obscured by the pressures and demands of our lives. Never mind the forest for the trees - we don't see the blessings for the bills! But every once in awhile, it catches us by surprise. We are moved by beauty. It is a gentle reminder of God's presence. Maybe it's a dandelion growing through a crack in the sidewalk – a sign that life is meant to be lived despite any obstacles. Maybe it is a neighbor's smile, or a beneficial "coincidence." In any case, our lives are beautiful, we are beautiful, even if we need to be reminded of it every once in awhile. *-Lissa Coffey*

"Beauty is truth, truth beauty – that is all
Ye know on earth, and all ye need to know."
-John Keats

We're always hearing new "definitions" of beauty – whether they are cultural or based on our own generation. But this simple statement explains it all so clearly. It's like the two words are interchangeable. The truth is what is, not what is not. Beauty is. God is. *-Lissa Coffey*

"I pray thee, O God, that I may be beautiful within."
-Socrates

Ah, Socrates! Wisdom is beautiful! You are beautiful! Who would argues that this great philosopher wasn't beautiful? It's like a supermodel wishing to be more photogenic. We are all beautiful simply because we ARE. We are here, on this beautiful planet. We cannot be MORE beautiful, because we are already all that. Yet we can recognize that beauty, cultivate it, cherish it. We can express beauty, and show gratitude for it. *-Lissa Coffey*

"Never lose an opportunity of seeing anything that
is beautiful; for beauty is God's handwriting – a
wayside sacrament. Welcome it in every fair face, in
every fair sky, in every fair flower, and thank God for
it as a cup of blessing."
-Ralph Waldo Emerson

Beauty is everywhere, all around an in each one of us. Yet where do we put our attention? On what we have decided is "wrong?" On what we think needs to be "fixed?" There is beauty in these things, too – if we would only look for it. There is a lesson, a gift, a treasure to be found in every situation and circumstance. We can acknowledge it or turn away from it – but it is there nonetheless. *-Lissa Coffey*

> "At some point in life the world's beauty becomes enough.
> You don't need to photograph, paint or even remember it.
> It is enough."
> -Toni Morrison

We always seem to be striving for MORE. More money, more time, more patience, more love... when we have so much and don't even know it. Or if we know it in the intellectual sense, we don't really believe it enough to live it. We have all of this abundance and more available to us – it is ours to claim and enjoy and celebrate! The beauty of our world, God's world, is in us and all around us at all times. At some point, we come to respect that, and appreciate it, and know that it is plenty enough. *-Lissa Coffey*

Beginnings & Endings

> "'Begin at the beginning.' the King said, gravely,
> 'and go till you come to the end; then stop.'"
> -Lewis Carroll (1832 - 1898) Alice's Adventures in Wonderland, 1865

Just where is this "beginning?" It's an arbitrary thing. There is no real beginning, and there is no real end. Remember when it was New Year's 2000 and the big argument was whether the New Millennium started on January 1, 2000 or January 1, 2001? And there was this huge concern about Y2K? It all seems so silly now. Each day is another day. We can choose when our beginnings are. We can begin right here, right now, right where we are. Or we can wait until tomorrow! It's our choice, not the calendar's or the clock's. *-Lissa Coffey*

> "We shall not cease from exploration
> And the end of all our exploring
> Will be to arrive where we started
> And know the place for the first time."
> -T.S. Eliot (1888-1965)

There is a phrase we often use about "coming full circle" meaning that we've ended up back where we started, but with a newfound knowledge. Life is not linear. Some say it is like a spiral, others say it is like a ball of yarn. We go around seeing things and people and experiences that we've seen before, but we see them with new eyes because we have more understanding as we grow. *-Lissa Coffey*

"There will come a time when you believe everything is finished. That will be the beginning."
-Louis L'Amour (1908-1988)

We're finishing up the current year, it is coming to an end. And as we head into a new year, we think about new beginnings. Endings and beginnings are a natural progression. This year my son Brian got his black belt in karate. It was the culmination of many years of learning. It was through much persistence and hard work that he earned that belt. And yet, as much as the black belt represents an ending, an accomplishment, an achievement - it also represents a beginning. Black belt means "master of the basics" - it means that the real work has just begun. There is always more to learn. *-Lissa Coffey*

"Every exit is... an entrance somewhere else."
-Tom Stoppard

This sounds like an optimistic way of looking at things. It's the same as "when one door closes, another one opens." But it's so true. Look at the opportunities that arise when something ends. All that energy has to go somewhere - so new situations and circumstances are created. It's exciting! Change is good. Beginnings are good. *-Lissa Coffey*

"The way to achieve a difficult thing was to set it in motion."
-Kate O'Brien, 1943

Just start. Just begin. Whatever it is we want to achieve, whatever our goals or resolutions may be - the most important thing we can do to make things happen is to take that first step. Then we can build up a momentum, and a drive, and an excitement as we approach what once seemed to be so far off. If it is in our mind, it can be within our reach if we just begin. *-Lissa Coffey*

Belief

"Believe that you may understand."
-St. Augustine (A.D. 354 - 430)

Belief is the first step toward understanding, which then leads to knowledge, wisdom, faith, and conviction. Belief suggests that we are to trust something that we can't necessarily see. We have to take someone's word for it. Or we have to trust our own inner vision that something is possible which hasn't happened yet. Belief takes strength, and it can help us to grow. *-Lissa Coffey*

"Believe in something larger than yourself."
-Barbara Bush

We often hear: "Believe in yourself." I don't know if it's all that easy sometimes. But when we have trouble believing in ourselves, when we have doubts, we can always believe in that something larger than ourselves. There's that spirit, that energy, that "Something" to which we are all connected, and from which we draw our strength, that keeps us going. *-Lissa Coffey*

"Some things have to be believed to be seen."
-Ralph Hodgson (1871 - 1962)

Skeptics say: "I'll believe it when I see it." But belief often works the other way around - we see it when we believe it! What is the criteria for manifesting something? It starts with believing, knowing, asserting that which we want to be true. Ah, and then it happens - and we see that we were right all along! There is power in belief. *-Lissa Coffey*

"To believe in something not yet proved and to under-write it with our lives: it is the only way we can leave the future open."
-Lillian Smith, The Journey (1954)

Wow. Think of all the people throughout history who have done just that. And that is why we are where we are today! The Wright brothers believe in flight - something not yet proven. Alexander Graham Bell believed in communicating over wires. Steve Jobs and Bill Gates believed that a crazy thing called a computer belonged in everyone's house! All of these people took risks, they underwrote their beliefs with their lives. And thank goodness they did! The future is wide open.
-Lissa Coffey

"All things are possible to him who believes."
-Jesus, Mark 9:23

It's as simple and as beautiful as this statement. All things are possible to him who believes. Believes what? To him who believes that all things are possible! Believe that all things are possible and they are! Believe that things are impossible and they are! We can choose what we believe. I believe in infinite possibilities! *-Lissa Coffey*

"You gotta believe."
-Tug McGraw (1944)

Tug McGraw played baseball for the New York Mets. In the 1973 National League pennant race, he would repeat this saying over and over again to his team. It became a kind of mantra for him. What he meant with those little words was: we can do this, we can win this, know it in your heart, see it, believe it! And it worked. The Mets went from 5th place to 1st place that year, and won the pennant! *-Lissa Coffey*

Birth

"Man's main task in life is to give birth to himself."
-Erich Fromm (1900-1980)

This is it. It's like the butterfly. First it is given birth as a caterpillar. And then it transforms, it gives birth to itself as a butterfly. We are very much the same. We are born into this body, and then we discover who we really are, we transform ourselves into who we want to be. And then we can fly. *-Lissa Coffey*

"Birth may be a matter of a moment. But it is a unique one."
-Frederick Leboyer

Birth is a beginning. It is the single event that starts us on our journey in this lifetime. Our grand entrance into the world! And here we are. Somehow all the right pieces were in place to make this miracle, and we were born to live this life. Life is precious. *-Lissa Coffey*

"Our birth is but a sleep and a forgetting."
-William Wordsworth (1770-1850)

We are in human form, but we are spiritual beings. We need to awaken to that, and remain aware of our spirituality. The body demands attention, and we must take good care of it. With a healthy body we are more free to learn and grow and experience more of the spiritual, more of ourselves. *-Lissa Coffey*

**"I have learned to judge of men by their own deeds,
and not to make the accident of birth the standard of
their merit."**
- Sarah J. Hale (1790-1879)

We are not our name, or our address, or our inherited position or any other label that comes with our birth. We are far more than that. And that discovery of Self is the great journey that each of us end up on at various times in our lives. We are here to learn and to grow and to contribute in our own unique way. *-Lissa Coffey*

**"I was so surprised at being born that I didn't speak
for a year and a half."**
-Gracie Allen (1932)

Look at these little babies, little wise souls just new to this earth. How sweet and precious and rare. Sometimes when I meet someone I think about what they must have been like as a child. Children are innocent, and that child-like innocence remains within us somewhere, we just don't let everyone see it. *-Lissa Coffey*

Blessings

"Yes, there is a Nirvanah: it is in leading your sheep to
a green pasture, and in putting your child to sleep, and
in writing the last line of your poem."
-Kahlil Gibran

Our blessings are right in front of us, every day. The little things that make us happy, those are the things that make life worthwhile. It's easy to see the big blessings, they get our attention - but the sweet, simple, small events that make us smile, for those we must be grateful, too. -*Lissa Coffey*

"Good heavens, of what uncostly material is our
earthly happiness composed... if we only knew it.
What incomes have we not had from a flower, and
how unfailing are the dividends of the seasons."
-James Russell Lowell

Blessings have no monetary value, and yet, they're priceless! We're showered with an abundance of nature and love, a bounty of blessings just waiting to be harvested with our hearts. Indulge! -*Lissa Coffey*

"The best things are nearest: breath in your nostrils,
light in your eyes, flowers at your feet, duties at your
hand, the path of God just before you. Then do not
grasp at the stars, but do life's plain, common work as
it comes, certain that daily duties and daily bread are
the sweetest things of life."
-Robert Louis Stevenson

Stevenson says "do not grasp at the stars" as if to say- don't worry so much about things you don't have, things that are out of your reach. Instead, focus on the task at hand, and see the beauty and the blessings which are right here, right now. We can't appreciate what is right in front of us if we are looking off into the distance. -*Lissa Coffey*

"Just to be is a blessing. Just to live is holy."
-Abraham Heschel

Think of the odds, think of what it took to get us here, in this particular body, at this particular time. So many events had to occur exactly the way that they did for us to exist right now. What if your mother hadn't met your father? The "what ifs" are endless! But somehow everything fell into place miraculously to create this life that you're living. So now we're here - and what we gain from this experience, how we learn and grow and make this blessing really count, is all up to us! -*Lissa Coffey*

> **"Life is the first gift, love is the second, and understanding the third."**
> -Marge Piercy

We accept the first gift just by being born. We learn more of the second gift all throughout our life, and we give and receive love. The third gift seems to be more of a challenge for us to accept. We tend to want to impose our interpretations, our judgements on circumstances and behaviors rather than seeking to understand. It takes a certain spiritual maturity to really let go embrace this blessing. We have this capacity- let's unwrap this gift! *-Lissa Coffey*

Body

> **"We should conduct ourselves not as if we ought to live for the body, but as if we could not live without it."**
> -Seneca the Younger (5? BC – AD 65)

There is a kind of mindfulness that we need to observe when taking care of the body. We need to exercise, but not overdo. We need to eat properly, but not too much. This is a precious package that is ours to take care of. And when we take care of the body, it takes care of us. We all have this in common. We may look so different on the outside – different shapes, sizes, colors, ages, whatever. But on the inside– it's all the same basic equipment. What makes us "tick" is all the same "stuff." *-Lissa Coffey*

> **"If anything is sacred, the human body is sacred."**
> -Walt Whitman (1819-1892)

The body really is such a miracle. It's just beyond comprehension how all of our organs can work so effortlessly on our behalf to keep us up and running. We don't have to think about breathing, or pumping blood – it just happens! Life is so precious. The body is its keeper. It's up to us to nourish and nurture this sacred vessel so that we may wisely use our time on earth learning and growing. The more time that we're here, the more time that we have to expand our awareness. Our bodies allow us to do that. *-Lissa Coffey*

> **"The body is shaped, disciplined, honored, and in time, trusted."**
> -Martha Graham, Blood Memory, 1991

Dancers know, as Martha Graham so beautifully states, that our bodies respond to the attention that we give them. When we take care of the body with nutrition and exercise and personal care, we can trust the body to function optimally. *-Lissa Coffey*

> **"The body says what words cannot."**
> -Martha Graham, 1985

"Movement never lies."
-Martha Graham, Blood Memory 1991

We express ourselves with our bodies. Our body "language" tells things about us that we cannot hide. Our emotions are broadcast to the world through our posture and our physicality. Our bodies are our instruments – and we can play them with dance and athletics and joy! -*Lissa Coffey*

"The body is wiser than its inhabitants. The body is the soul. We ignore its aches, its pains, its eruptions, because we fear the truth. The body is God's messenger."
-Erica Jong, Fear of Fifty, 1994

The body definitely gives us signals, but do we pay attention? We should! Look at all we can learn from the body! It tells us when we're tired, under stress, hungry, nervous. We may try to fight it, or ignore it, thinking we know better – but there is an innate intelligence at work in our cells that we can benefit from. This "gut instinct" that we get, that's Spirit talking right to us. Listen up! -*Lissa Coffey*

Business

"One of the best ways to persuade others is with your ears – by listening to them."
-Dean Rusk

We have two ears, and one mouth. It's easy for us to close our mouth, but unless we use earplugs or our hands, we can't really close our ears. Isn't that telling? We are meant to listen. We can learn so much just by being still and taking in the information that we are given. Everyone wants to be heard. Give the gift of listening. -*Lissa Coffey*

"To business that we love we rise betime, And go to it with delight."
-Shakespeare, "Antony and Cleopatra"

It's the best feeling to do work that we love. It doesn't feel like "work" at all! Time flies. We feel fulfilled, and satisfied. When we love what we do, and we are helping people at the same time, that's when we know we are in our dharma, or purpose in life. -*Lissa Coffey*

"You are never giving, nor can you ever give, enough service."
-James R. Cook

There is always more that we can do to help. Opportunities are around us every day. At the grocery store, on the sidewalk, in cyberspace, at school or at work. We are here to help each other, every day in every way. When we just open up our awareness, we can see where we are needed. Every business is a service business. *-Lissa Coffey*

"Whenever you see a successful business, someone once made a courageous decision."
-Peter Drucker

There are times when it is best to take baby steps, to move cautiously. And then there are times when we need to take a leap of faith and just go for it. Starting a business is a big decision in itself. And like life, and everything else, how much we put into it shows. Success is a personal definition, it's about how you feel. *-Lissa Coffey*

"All business proceeds on beliefs, on judgments of probabilities, and not on certainties."
-Charles W. Eliot

Let's look at this in terms of business in the broadest sense. For example, we are all running the business of our lives. We're the CEO. Many of the same principles that apply to running a business then apply to us in this way. There are no certainties in life – we make decisions based on what we've learned so far, and maybe a little bit of intuition. *-Lissa Coffey*

Cause and Effect

"What is found in the effect was already in the cause."
-Henri Bergson (1859-1941)

We've heard it before – we reap what we sow. What we sow (cause) is what we reap (effect). Our energy generates something that comes back to us. Our efforts, or actions, cause things to happen, so we need to be mindful of what we say and do. And really, the effect becomes another cause, which produces another effect! It's easy to use the analogy of gardening: we plant a tomato seed, which grows tomatoes, which produce tomato seeds. What is found in the tomato was already in the seed, and vice versa. The seed holds the potential for the tomato. We can apply the same knowledge to our lives, and create for ourselves the love and joy that we want to experience just by sowing the seeds for that. *-Lissa Coffey*

"Every chemical substance, every plant, every animal in its growth, teaches the unity of cause, the variety of appearance."
-Ralph Waldo Emerson (1803-1882)

Biologically, look at all we have in common with every other mammal. And yet, it seems as though our path is much different than that of the cow, or the tiger. But we are born to a mother, just like our animal friends, and we go through life learning and growing. The cause is the same; the effect is the same. We can learn from examples in nature that we truly are all one, there are no real differences between us. *-Lissa Coffey*

"Curiosity, or love of the knowledge of causes, draws a man from consideration of the effect to seek the cause; and again, the cause of that cause, till of necessity he must come to this thought at last, that there is some cause, whereof there is no former cause, but is eternal, which – men call God."
-Thomas Hobbes (1588-1679)

We are compelled to learn. It is in our nature. We can't help it. And the more we learn, the more that knowledge brings us to ourselves. We look outside, we read, we study, we work – and what we learn is to look inside. We look inside to turn knowledge into wisdom, and we grow. *-Lissa Coffey*

"In the spiritual life, every cause is also an effect, and
every effect is at the same time a cause."
-Aldous Huxley (1894-1963)

What came first? We don't know what came first because there is no beginning, and there is no end. What is real is eternal, and timeless. And even though there is no timeline, there is perfect order, perfect organization, definite purpose. So here we are, a part of it all, a cause and also an effect. *-Lissa Coffey*

"Between cause and its so-called effect there falls, as it
were, a cosmic shadow and out of this shadow man can
accomplish a transfiguration of his own, participating,
however minutely, in an act of universal creation, and
something effective that no cause all alone and purely
out of itself could have produced."
-Laurens van der Post (1906-1996)

We are a created and we create. We have access to all the wisdom and power of the Universe. Our potential for creativity is unlimited. Opportunities abound! Are we awake to this? Are we actively participating in the process? Whether it's "Carpe Diem" or "Go for it," it is important to take action in our own causes and effects. Choose consciously. *-Lissa Coffey*

Challenge

"To be tested is good. The challenged life may be the
best therapist."
-Gail Sheehy, 1986

So here's our challenge. Every day is a new day, a new start. What shall we do with ourselves? I know, we're busy people, we have enough to do. But are we challenging ourselves? Are we learning and growing and stretching ourselves to do the best that we can every day? It doesn't matter what we do so much as how we go about doing it. We meet a challenge by going for it! *-Lissa Coffey*

"Providence has hidden a charm in difficult undertakings,
which is appreciated only by those who dare to grapple
with them."
-Anne-Sophie Swetchine, 1869

Ah! Doesn't this explain it! When we accept a challenge, work through it to the other side, then we understand and appreciate the growth that comes as our reward. It's easy to shrug off a challenge, to think that it's too big of a risk, that it could be a waste of our time. But to tackle a challenge, to grapple with it, leads us to a place where we discover just what we are capable of, and that is beautiful. *-Lissa Coffey*

"You must do the thing you think you cannot do."
-Eleanor Roosevelt, 1960

This is the thing – it's not that we cannot do it, it's that we think we cannot do it. That is why we MUST do it. Sometimes we just have to prove to ourselves, to remind ourselves, that we can do anything we set our minds to. We are intelligent, capable, remarkable beings. What can you do? Anything! *-Lissa Coffey*

"When people keep telling you that you can't do a thing, you kind of like to try it."
-Margaret Chase Smith, 1964

I guess this is a little like reverse psychology. When we are kids, if someone says "I dare you" it's like a challenge that we can't resist. Sometimes a challenge is just what we need to spur us on to what we really need to do for ourselves and our personal growth. Maybe it's because we know someone is watching, that someone will notice. That's just a part of being human. Whatever works! *-Lissa Coffey*

"The fruit that can fall without shaking, Indeed is too mellow for me."
-Lady Mary Wortley Montagu, 1803

There are a lot of analogies along these lines. "Go our on a limb, that's where the fruit is!" The fruit that falls is ready and ripe – but it is ready and ripe before it falls. Sometimes a little shake is just what it needs to get it where it needs to be! Otherwise it might rot on the vine. As people, we get a little bit comfortable where we are, we're happy to "hang around," maybe longer than we should. Sometimes a challenge, a little shake-up, gets us going. *-Lissa Coffey*

Chance

"Chance is always powerful. Let your hook be always cast. In the pool where you least expect it, will be a fish."
-Ovid

Are we ready for opportunity when it presents itself? We don't have x-ray vision, we can't see around corners, but good things are always there for us at every turn. We can make the most of chance by being prepared to say "yes!" *-Lissa Coffey*

"Where observation is concerned, chance favors only the prepared mind."
-Louis Pasteur, 1854

Sometimes we get ourselves into such a routine that we lose our power of observation. We don't see the forest for the trees, so to speak! But when we open up our vision, expand our awareness, we start to see patterns. And then we see that things are not so random at all. We can prepare ourselves, and make what seems like "chance" work in our favor. *-Lissa Coffey*

> **"There is no such thing as chance; and what seems to us the merest accident springs from the deepest source of destiny."**
> -Johann Christoph Friedrich von Schiller (1759-1805)

Sometimes when we look at something very close up, it doesn't make sense. Like when you have just one piece of the puzzle, you can't figure out what the whole picture is. But then when we pull back it all comes into perspective, we see how everything "fits" together. Everything happens for a reason, we're all here for a reason. It might not make sense to us, but as time goes on and things fall into place, we see the big picture – and we see that it is beautiful. *-Lissa Coffey*

> **"What can be more foolish than to think that all this rare fabric of heaven and earth could come by chance, when all the skill of art is not able to make an oyster!"**
> -Jeremy Taylor (1613-1667)

Is there such a thing as chance, or coincidence, or serendipity? Or is everything carefully orchestrated and organized by a Higher Power? Chance seems to be the unexpected, but then we have to think: who is doing the expecting? Something might come as a surprise to us, but it might also have been planned in the cosmos since before time. *-Lissa Coffey*

> **"A wise man turns Chance into good Fortune."**
> -Thomas Fuller (1654-1734)

When we have that chance, that opportunity that we've been looking for, the opportunity that we actually create for ourselves, we've got to move on it. We make our good fortune by the opportunities we take. *-Lissa Coffey*

Change

> **"Everything is connected... no one thing can change by itself."**
> -Paul Hawken

There is so much simplicity, and so much truth in this statement. Through the internet, we are connected with people from all over the world. We may not seem to have anything else in common, but we are reading the same words this morning. The internet has made the world much smaller, so that we can experience our connection with each other more tangibly!

And as we each experience our own spiritual growth, we affect change in our world.

Little by little, one by one, we are making a difference. And as the world changes, it inspires us as we see the possibilities, and we continue on our journey. *-Lissa Coffey*

"The people who are crazy enough to think they can change the world are the ones who do."
-Apple computer TV ad

The world is changing... and we are changing the world by our actions whether we realize it or not. Just a thought can change things, make things better. So the idea is that the more people who are growing spiritually, the more people who are consciously seeking this change, this improvement to our world, the more easily and quickly this change will occur. It's happening already. *-Lissa Coffey*

"Let us suppose that there are two sorts of existences – one seen, the other unseen... The seen is the changing, and the unseen is the unchanging."
-Socrates (470?-399 B.C.)

We see change everyday. We see it in the seasons, the weather, in our rapidly growing children! The nature of life is to grow, and in that growth is change. And then there is the constant in our lives, the one thing that is always there, unseen, yet unchanging, and that is Spirit. As we go about our busy lives, adjusting to the changes that occur all around us, we can find comfort and peace in the stillness knowing that this is where all of life, all of creation, is connected. *-Lissa Coffey*

"Things do not change; we change."
-Henry David Thoreau (1817-1862)

When we change our perspective, things look differently to us. We may think that they have changed, but it is really our point of view that has changed. We tend to put our own labels and definitions on things, yet those change when we see things a different way. The value that we put on things changes, too. And isn't it all just this subjective, arbitrary notion? Different people will have different opinions, that's just the way it is... and yet, the "thing," whatever it is, is what it is. Opening up our minds to other people's perspectives allows us to change and grow and become more accepting and understanding. *-Lissa Coffey*

"A person can run for years but sooner or later he has to take a stand in the place which, for better or worse, he calls home, do what he can to change things there."
-Paule Marshall (1969)

It is our nature, and really our responsibility, to change things for the better. Some causes resonate with us, we are compelled to help, we can't help it. Some causes come to us – through an illness, or a friend or relative whom we love. There is always some way we can invoke change, some way we can make a difference. When something moves you, go with it as an opportunity to learn and grow, and change the world. *-Lissa Coffey*

Character

"The great hope of society is individual character."
-William Ellery Channing (1780-1842)

We each carry with us the hope of the world. We each make a difference. Every action we take reveals our character. We must deliberately and intentionally strive to make this world a better place. And we will --one by one. -*Lissa Coffey*

"It is not in the still calm of life, or the repose of a
pacific station, that great characters are formed...
The habits of a vigorous mind are formed in contending with
difficulties. All history will convince you of this, and
that wisdom and penetration are the fruit of experience,
not the lessons of retirement and leisure. Great necessities
call out great virtues."
-Abigail Adams, in a letter to her son, John Quincy Adams, 1780

"Character" is an interesting word. We're all known for our character, those traits that we have embraced and exhibited as a part of who we are. In the movie and theatre world, a character is one of the participants in the film, or play – and since we have little time to get to know that individual, his personality is amplified by a few traits that sets him apart from the other characters. If you were to write a play, and write yourself into this story, how would your character be portrayed? -*Lissa Coffey*

"Character cannot be developed in ease and quiet.
Only through experiences of trial and suffering can
the soul be strengthened, vision cleared, ambition
inspired and success achieved."
-Helen Keller, 1938

Everything that we have gone through in our lives has come to shape our character. How we assimilate these experiences into our personality determines the strength of our character. Life is not easy – and it's not boring! Every day offers us up opportunities to learn and grow and develop into the person we aspire to be. -*Lissa Coffey*

"The world may take your reputation from you, but it
cannot take your character."
-Emma Dunham Kelley, Megda, 1891

"A man's character is the reality of himself.
His reputation is the opinion others have formed of him.
Character is in him; reputation is from other people –
that is the substance, this is the shadow."
-H.W. Beecher (1813-1887)

> ### "If I take care of my character, my reputation will take care of itself."
> -D.L. Moody (1837-1899)

I just had to include all three of these quotes together. These were taken from three different sources! I don't know if these people knew each other, or were commenting on their statements – but it sure sounds like it. That's the way spirit works sometimes – all these events happening in different times and places that somehow mesh together seamlessly. Notice the contrast that each draws between character and reputation. Where do we place the most value?

There are things we can work on, and things we really have no control over. When we work on ourselves, the rest seems to fall into place. It's the "reap what you sow" factor taken to another level. It's the "ripple effect" that we can't always see because we're right in the middle of it. *-Lissa Coffey*

> ### "Character building begins in our infancy and continues until death."
> -Eleanor Roosevelt

Every day our characters are formed by the choices we make. What do we think about? How do we spend our time? What do we value? Our characters are a reflection of our life lessons. How well have we learned? *-Lissa Coffey*

Children

> ### "We find a delight in the beauty and happiness of children that makes the heart too big for the body."
> -Ralph Waldo Emerson (1803-1882)

This Christmas week we turn our attention to children, and the joy and delight we find as we see the season through their eyes. One bright and glorious morning, more than two thousand years ago, a little child was born who would change the world. And that same possibility is born in each of us. We can change the world. Each child new to this world can make this a better place for all of us. Let us open our hearts to each other, all the children of the world. *-Lissa Coffey*

> ### "Remember the feeling as a child when you woke up and morning smiled, it's time you felt like that again."
> -Taj Mahal, "Take a Giant Step" (song, 1969)

There's nothing like the child-like joy of Christmas morning! Everything is new and fresh and waiting to be unwrapped by eager little hands. Life can be like that every day. The world awaits us, and we approach, uncertain of what we will find in store for us. Each day is a present, filled with present moments. Indulge! Merry Christmas! *-Lissa Coffey*

"No day can be so sacred but that the laugh of a little
child will make it holier still."
-Robert G. Ingersoll (1833-1899), "Liberty of Man, Woman and Child" 1898

There are so many lessons we can learn from children! The innocence, the open-heartedness, the sheer joy of discovery. Time spent with children is blessed time indeed. Where did our child-like nature go? We can find it again in shapes of the clouds, in a toasted marshmallow, or a shared giggle. -*Lissa Coffey*

"Every child comes with the message that God is not
yet discouraged of man."
-Rabindranath Tagore (1861-1941) Stray Birds, 1914

Every child holds a promise, every child IS a promise - a glimpse of what life is all about. Who doesn't melt when holding a tiny baby? Our hearts fill with awe at the sight of this spectacular little being. It's a miracle. Each one of us is that miracle, too. We are still children, learning and growing and finding our way. -*Lissa Coffey*

"Children are God's apostles, day by day
Sent forth to preach of love, and hope, and peace."
-James Russell Lowell (1819-1891)

There's a saying: "out of the mouths of babes" because children tend to speak the truth so clearly, just when we need to hear it. Are we listening? Are we getting the messages of love, and hope, and peace? We can learn so much from our children, and all children are our children, because we are all one. -*Lissa Coffey*

Choice

"The strongest principle of growth lies in human choice."
-George Eliot, 1874

We make choices all the time, pretty much every moment of every day. We choose when to get up, what to wear, what to eat. And we make big choices, too – whom to marry, where to live, how to live. Every choice we've made up until now has brought us to this point in time. We have learned from our choices, and we have grown. Where do we go from here? It's our choice. -*Lissa Coffey*

"Choice is the essence of what I believe it is to be human."
-Liv Ullmann, 1984

Some people might say that choice is free will. We exercise our free will by making the choice that we feel is best for us at the time. We always have a choice. Sometimes it doesn't feel like it, but we do. We might need to get creative to see the possibilities, but once we do we see that life is a banquet, it's like an all-you-can-eat buffet! Choose wisely, choose well. -*Lissa Coffey*

"To choose is also to begin."
-Starhawk, 1982

That's it. The first step is always to make a choice. Pick one, whether it's a color, or a flavor, or a career, or a path. And go for it. That's not to say that we can't pick again. We can always choose again. But we've got to start somewhere. *-Lissa Coffey*

**"God offers to every mind its choice between
truth and repose."**
-Ralph Waldo Emerson (1803-1882)

I looked up "repose" to make sure I understood this quote. In my dictionary "repose" means "sleep." Now this makes sense. If repose is sleep, then truth is being awake, being aware. It is our choice to wake up! And here we are, learning and growing and contributing. We've chosen truth. Good choice! *-Lissa Coffey*

"Guess if you can, choose if you dare."
-Pierre Corneille

Sometimes making a choice is being courageous. It's movement forward. It's going ahead. When we can't choose we're stuck, and immobile. Once we choose then action can take place. And then as things happen we'll have more choices to make. That's just natural progression. We can adjust, we can learn, and choosing makes that possible. *-Lissa Coffey*

Collaboration

**"There are three ways of dealing with difference:
domination, compromise, and integration. By domination
only one side gets what it wants; by compromise neither
side gets what it wants; by integration we find a way
by which both sides may get what they wish."**
-Mary Parker Follett

A certain energy is generated when people work together. And many times the total outcome is greater than the sum of the parts. We each have something to contribute. We can put our heads together, and our talents together, and come up with solutions to all kinds of challenges. *-Lissa Coffey*

**"Every time a man unburdens his heart to a stranger
he reaffirms the love that unites humanity."**
-Germaine Greer

There is a certain trust that comes with collaboration. We allow our ideas to be heard, we put our hearts on the line hoping for some clarification, or feedback, that we are going in the right direction. Collaboration is coming together with a common goal. *-Lissa Coffey*

**"Good communication is as stimulating as black coffee,
and just as hard to sleep after."**
-Anne Morrow Lindbergh

Collaboration can be so exciting! When ideas get bandied about and the creativity flows, so much energy is created! It gets us going, it's encouraging and motivating when we feel heard and understood. And then watching the project come together, knowing that we had a hand in it, is just wonderful. *-Lissa Coffey*

"Exchange is creation."
-Muriel Rukeyser

The creative process is fascinating. Everyone goes about it in his own way, but in almost every case, creation does not happen alone. People give us ideas, inspiration, encouragement and support. There's an exchange of energy that makes things happen, or allows things to happen. We're better for it, and our projects are better for it.
-Lissa Coffey

**"When two people are writing the same book, each
believes he gets all the worries and only half the royalties."**
-Agatha Christie (1955)

I think this pretty much applies in any business! And pretty much at times in any relationship. What we're looking for is balance. Very rarely is the division of labor split 50/50. Life just doesn't work like that. Sometimes in one area it's 80/20, or in another it's 40/60. It is important that we contribute to the best of our ability at any given time. Overall, a successful collaboration is where all of the parties involved can look at a finished project and say that they would do it again. *-Lissa Coffey*

Colors

**"Green is the fresh emblem of well-founded hopes.
In blue the spirit can wander, but in green it can rest."**
-Mary Webb, The Spring of Joy, 1917

We live in this colorful world and I think we sometimes take that for granted. So let's put our attention on colors just a little bit and see what we can learn from their presence in our lives. Green brings to mind growth – all the green grass, green moss, it is cool and restful. Green also represents growth in terms of money, financial growth. But then we also say that we can be "green with envy" and that's not such a good thing! There's also the gardener who has a "green thumb" – and I remember Mr. Green Jeans on Captain Kangaroo! What comes to mind when you think of green? Emeralds, Ireland... let your imagination wander a little! *-Lissa Coffey*

> "Red has been praised for its nobility of the color of life.
> But the true color of life is not red. Red is the color of
> violence, or of life broken open, edited, and published."
> -Alice Meynell, The Color of Life, 1896

I don't think there are any "bad" colors – just different emotions and connotations that we associate with them, just like we do with anything else. Red it interesting that way- it's vibrant and bold – and yet can signal danger, and heat. Like anything, it's our own perception that we impose on it. *-Lissa Coffey*

> "I had forgotten what mustard fields looked like...
> Sheet upon sheet of blazing yellow, half-way between
> sulphur and celandrine, with hot golden sunshine
> pouring down upon them out of a dazzling June sky.
> It thrilled me like music."
> -Monica Baldwin, I Leap Over the Wall, 1950

The first thing that comes to mind when I think about yellow is the sun – beautiful, life-affirming, skin warming sunshine! I also think about old-fashioned wooden pencils and school buses – and sunflowers! It's really a happy color, isn't it? Yellow seems to be attention-getting, and in color therapy, it is used to harness attention. Wearing a citrine, for example, is supposed to help you concentrate. And whoever invented the original Post-It notes must have made them yellow for a reason! If this were written in color, I'd send a bright yellow happy face today! *-Lissa Coffey*

> "Of all colors, brown is the most satisfying. It is the
> deep, fertile tint of the earth itself; it lies hidden
> beneath every field and garden; it is the garment of
> multitudes of earth's children, from the mouse to the eagle."
> -Mary Webb, The Spring of Joy, 1917

Brown isn't one of the colors in the rainbow- and yet, could you imagine a world without it? To me, brown represents nature – tree trunks, dirt, things that are real. And chocolate! No, I couldn't imagine a world without it... *-Lissa Coffey*

> "Black was bestlooking... Ebony was the best wood,
> the hardest wood; it was black. Virginia ham was the
> best ham. It was black on the outside. Tuxedos and
> tail coats were black and they were a man's finest, most
> expensive clothes. You had to use pepper to make most
> meats and vegetables fit to eat. The most flavorsome
> pepper was black. The best caviar was black. The rarest
> jewels were black: black opals, black pearls."
> -Ann Petry, The Narrows, 1953

Black is elegant, and mysterious. Black is often said to be the absence of color, but I think it deserves a place as a color itself. The fashion world certainly couldn't function without it! Maybe black has gotten a bad rap because it is associated with the villain's hat – but black, like white, is like a canvas, and we can paint on it most vividly! *-Lissa Coffey*

Comfort

"I have enjoyed many of the comforts of life, none of
which I wish to esteem lightly; yet I confess I know not
any joy that is so dear to me, that so fully satisfies the
inmost desires of my mind, that so enlivens refines, and
elevates my whole nature, as that which I derive from
religion – from faith in God. – May this God be thy God,
thy refuge, thy comfort, as he has been mine."
-John Caspar Lavater (1741-1801)

It doesn't matter which religion we follow – we can garner comfort from our relationship with God, from our faith. When we feel in need of comfort, this is where we should turn first. Out of habit, we tend to look elsewhere – but we will always find comfort, and strength when we look within. *-Lissa Coffey*

"I love it – I love it; and who shall dare
To chide me for loving that old arm-chair?"
-Eliza Cook, 1848

There's no place like home! Was it Dorothy in the Wizard of Oz who first said that? Whenever I travel I always find myself appreciating so much the comforts of home upon my return. There's just something about the familiarity of it all that is so reassuring, so cozy! It's nice to have things around us with which we have some history.
-Lissa Coffey

"Give me a well-cooked, well-served meal, a bouquet, and
a sunset, and I can do more for a man's soul than all the
cant ever preached. I can even do it without a sunset!"
-Anne Ellis, 1929

With Mother's Day coming up on Sunday, I thought this quote was particularly appropriate. Is there anyone more comforting that Mom? I don't think so! When a child is hurt, he wants his mother. When an athlete waves to the camera, he says "Hi, Mom!" We are each and every one of us our mother's children. That never changes, and in that we can find comfort. *-Lissa Coffey*

"One sits uncomfortably on a too comfortable cushion."
-Lillian Hellman, 1976

What I get from this is that there is such a thing as "too comfortable" and that's not necessarily a good thing. We need a certain amount of change, and renewal in our lives to keep things moving, to keep things active. Life spurs us on – and one way it does that is by making us uncomfortable sometimes. We feel the need to seek comfort, and that causes us to grow. *-Lissa Coffey*

> "I simply cannot understand the passion that some people
> have for making themselves thoroughly uncomfortable
> and then boasting about it afterwards."
> -Patricia Moyes, 1961

This passion seems to be particularly prevalent today – you can see it on "Survivor" and "Fear Factor" and shows like that. So what's the spiritual message here? I guess we could look at it several different ways – but let's choose one: When we challenge ourselves, and break outside of our comfort zone, we discover things about ourselves and reap rewards!-*Lissa Coffey*

Commitment

> "If you don't make a total commitment to whatever
> you're doing, then you start looking to bail out the first
> time the boat starts leaking. It's tough enough getting
> that boat to shore with everybody rowing, let alone
> when a guy stand up and starts putting his life jacket on."
> -Lou Holtz

Lou Holtz is the well-known football coach, and he's talking about teamwork, and the importance of commitment to the team. The analogy he uses is great because it's so visual – and you can see how one person's lack of commitment affects those around him.

On this Thanksgiving Day I think about the commitment our ancestors made when coming to this country. Can you imagine the courage it took to leave home for somewhere, something unknown – the possibility of something better? Once they set out in that "boat" there was no turning back. If we could only have that courage, that commitment, in our own lives to just "go for it!" Yes, there are risks – that comes with the territory, but like another saying goes: "no risks, no rewards!"
-*Lissa Coffey*

> One's lifework, I have learned, grows with the working
> and the living. Do it as if your life depended on it, and
> the first thing you know, you'll have made a life out of
> it. A good life, too."
> -Theresa Helburn

Lifework. Isn't all of life work at times?! Commitment does take work, but because we get so much out of what we put into it, it becomes a pleasure. Our relationships need attention, and the ones that get it help us to grow. Our lives are built on our commitments – to ourselves, our relationships, our work, and our communities.
-*Lissa Coffey*

> "Put your heart, mind, intellect and soul even to your
> smallest acts. This is the secret of success."
> -Swami Sivananda

Commitment is 100%. You can't hedge a little and say that you are committed. Your actions speak for themselves. Commitment is tied to so many other good things, like integrity – you say you will do something and then you do it, that's integrity, that's living up to your commitment. Commitment brings achievement, and success.
-Lissa Coffey

"I am seeking, I am striving, I am in it with all my heart."
-Vincent van Gogh

Are we committed to living life to its fullest? What does that mean to each one of us personally? How does that show up in our daily routines? I think what van Gogh was saying was that commitment has to be whole-hearted. Whatever it is, whether it's a friendship, a career, a marriage, or our spiritual pursuits – if we're in it with all our heart, then we're demonstrating the importance that it has in our lives. And whatever it is, will grow and bloom and thrive with our commitment to it. *-Lissa Coffey*

"If you don't wake up with something in your stomach every day that makes you think, "I want to make this movie," it'll never get made."
-Sherry Lansing

A commitment isn't something we have to talk ourselves into. It's identifying something we believe in so much, and want for ourselves so much, that it becomes a part of who we are. A commitment involves caring, and dedication, and loyalty beyond any distractions. *-Lissa Coffey*

Communication

"The whole art of life is knowing the right time to say things."
-Maeve Binchy

Communication is a term that is used to express the dialogue and understanding between people. There is definitely an art to this. It's not just what we say but how, and when, we say it. We need to be sensitive as to how our words are being interpreted. And communication is reciprocal, it is both giving and receiving. When we speak we are giving information, and receiving someone's attention. When we listen we are receiving information and giving our attention. *-Lissa Coffey*

"Listening is not merely not talking, though even that is beyond most of our powers; it means taking a vigorous, human interest in what is being told us."
-Alice Deur Miller

Communication works both ways. In order for one party to feel that they are being heard, and understood, the other party must actively listen. It's important that we give our full attention to the person speaking so that we can fully understand and appreciate what is being said. We just might learn something! *-Lissa Coffey*

"Silence is one of the great arts of conversation."
-Hannah Moore

There are times when we feel those "awkward pauses," when we want to fill up the empty space with words. But then there are those beautiful times when we are comfortable just sitting and being with another person, when silence adds to our experience. In Japanese watercolors, it is said that the strokes that are painted are just as important as the spaces that are left blank. The overall work is simple, elegant, and meaningful. *-Lissa Coffey*

"The strokes of the pen need deliberation as much as the sword needs swiftness."
-Julia Ward Howe

Communication is the written word as much as it is the spoken word. Just as we must think before we speak, it is important for us to put thought into any correspondence that we send out. We have so many choices with which words we use, and each word carries its own nuances. We need to think about our intent, and carry it through with our overall tone. *-Lissa Coffey*

"Violence of the tongue is very real – sharper than any knife."
-Mother Teresa

There's a child's song that says "sticks and stones may break my bones but words can never hurt me." Since most of us have been hurt by words, we know the truth is that words can be sharp, and our emotions can be fragile. The good news is that words can also be very healing, and loving. Our thoughtful communication can help a person to feel really good. *-Lissa Coffey*

Community

"People had changed - or rather fridges had changed them. Mrs. Munde felt that being able to store food for longer periods had broken down the community spirit. There was no need to share now, no need to meet every day, gathering your veg or killing a few rabbits."
-Jeannette Winterson, Boating for Beginners, 1985

Communities can form out of necessity, but also out of common interests or goals. Now we just seem to have more choices. We may not need community for our physical survival, but we do need it for our well-being. We gravitate toward each other, and to communities where we can help and support each other in various ways. *-Lissa Coffey*

"Perhaps no place in any community is so totally democratic as the town library. The only entrance requirement is interest."
-Lady Bird Johnson

While computers may be filled with information, and even provide online interactions with people around the globe, there's still no substitute for the local library. This is where we find knowledge, wisdom, comfort, and community. As much as things change, and become more high-tech, I hope that our books, and our libraries, will always be preserved. They offer a great service and easy accessibility for everyone. If you haven't been in a while, you might want to visit the library, explore, and see what surprises you can find. *-Lissa Coffey*

"Above all we need, particularly as children, the reassuring presence of a visible community, an intimate group that enfolds us with understanding and love, and that becomes an object of our spontaneous loyalty, as a criterion and point of reference for the rest of the human race."
-Lewis Mumford (1895-1990)

It helps us to know, from an early age, that we're not in this alone. We crave that love and support from other human beings. This is how we learn about people, and how we learn about ourselves. *-Lissa Coffey*

"There are no islands any more."
-Edna St. Vincent Millay, 1940

We can really see the connections between people and between communities more and more as we open our eyes to it. The internet is an interesting thing. In some ways it has isolated us, as we sit alone on our computers. But in many other ways, it has helped us to establish and build relationships with people, and to create communities that we otherwise may not have been a part of. It has opened up avenues of communication that hadn't existed before. *-Lissa Coffey*

"Snowflakes, leaves, humans, plants, raindrops, stars, molecules, microscopic entities all come in communities. The singular cannot in reality exist."
-Paula Gunn Allen, Grandmothers of the Light, 1991

When we think of the whole grand concept of "we are all one" - it's kind of a stepping stone to think first of our own communities. We belong to lots of little groups - our families, our neighborhoods, our clubs and organizations. And these communities all function because of the people involved with them! They become an entity unto themselves. They have a life of their own. And these smaller communities are all part of larger communities, too - which in turn interact and grow with others. It all starts with each of us as individuals, and expands to include the entire planet. *-Lissa Coffey*

Compassion

"What value has compassion that does not take its
object in its arms?"
-Antoine de Saint-Exupery (1900-1944)

Compassion at its best is active. We can feel someone's pain, and then we can actually do something to alleviate that pain. When we come together with compassion, our hearts join, and we feel our connection with Spirit and each other.
-Lissa Coffey

"It is the experience of touching the pain of others
that is the key to change... Compassion is a sign
of transformation."
-Jim Wallis

Compassion is not limited to the human experience. Although, as intelligent beings, we can understand and express compassion and extend comfort to one another. My friend Maryanne sent me an article about a herd of elephants who appeared to be mourning one of their own who had died. They cried. I don't know if elephants can understand with their minds just what they were experiencing, but they certainly were able to understand with their hearts. And we can empathize with them, we can project our own feelings of loss onto this situation and learn and grow from it.
-Lissa Coffey

"Compassion is the desire that moves the individual
self to widen the scope of its self-concern to embrace
the whole of the universal self."
-Arnold J. Toynbee (1889-1975)

Compassion moves us beyond our own immediate needs and concerns and shows us how important it is to look at the big picture. We are all in this together. When one of us feels pain it affects the whole. When one of us extends ourselves to ease that pain, the healing reverberates to affect the whole. *-Lissa Coffey*

"Spiritual energy brings compassion into the real
world. With compassion, we see benevolently our own
human condition and the condition of our fellow beings. We drop prejudice. We withhold judgment."
-Christina Baldwin (1990)

As the world grows spiritually, we will grow compassionately. The Bible tells the story of the Good Samaritan. We know this is an example for us to live by. If we would all practice compassion, follow our hearts to help others in need, then the real world would be a lot a lot less scary place to live. *-Lissa Coffey*

"The dew of compassion is a tear."
-George Gordon Noel Byron (1788-1824)

Compassion carries with it emotion. We feel it in our hearts. Compassion spurs us to action. It shows us the best of who we are, it allows us to move past our own issues and focus on the contribution we can make to our fellow human beings. *-Lissa Coffey*

Concentration

"To be able to concentrate for a considerable time is essential to difficult achievement."
-Bertrand Russell

We've heard this said hundreds of times, a hundred different ways. Don't give up. Keep your eye on the ball. Good things come to those who wait. Be patient. It's a philosophy that has been at the core of many grand achievements, as those who hang in there consider every failure merely another step toward their ultimate success. *-Lissa Coffey*

"If I have ever made any valuable discoveries, it has been owing more to patient attention than to any other talent."
-Isaac Newton

Guess what? WisdomNews is one year old now! And I could say the same thing that Isaac Newton said... We've had a full year's worth of messages, and I feel like it's just day by day, little by little, paying attention to all these wise people throughout time has helped us to make some valuable discoveries about ourselves. It's these little habits, these personal spiritual practices, that help us to concentrate on what really is important in life. Happy First Anniversary, everyone! *-Lissa Coffey*

"For him who has no concentration, there is no tranquility."
-Bhagavad Gita

I think about this a lot. I recently attended the CHADD conference – CHADD is for Children and Adults with Attention Deficit Disorders – and I know how difficult it can be to pay attention. But there are times when that attention, that focused concentration, can set us free! Whatever we focus on, we move towards. Whatever we think about, we become. So it is important to still the mind and choose our thoughts. Tranquility comes from that stillness, and from the knowingness that all is right with the world. *-Lissa Coffey*

"The secret of concentration is the secret of self-discovery. You reach inside yourself to discover your personal resources, and what it takes to match them to the challenge."
-Arnold Palmer

My friend Joe Buttita is a golf pro, and I thought of him when I saw this quote. I remember one time he was coaching my son I said: "He just needs to concentrate," and Joe said: "No, he just needs to relax and let it happen, you can't force it." Wise man! All of the teachings, the lessons, the practice – it becomes a part of us. There is a time to concentrate and learn, and there is a time to relax and let it happen. We know what to do. And when we quiet our minds we can do it! *-Lissa Coffey*

> "Choice of attention, to pay attention to this and
> ignore that, is to the inner life what choice of action
> is to the outer."
> -W.H. Auden

There are so many different things that command our attention every day. Radio stations, billboards, advertisements, television shows, politicians... our jobs, our families, our friends, our responsibilities... the list goes on and on. This is why our spiritual practices are so important. If we just listened to the news we would probably start living in fear. But when we balance our lives, and listen to our hearts, we can separate out what it is important to concentrate on. Keeping a routine of spiritual practice makes it easier for us to stay on the path. *-Lissa Coffey*

Confidence

> "Real confidence comes from knowing and accepting
> yourself -- your strengths and your limitations -- in
> contrast to depending on affirmation from others."
> -Judith M. Bardwick, 1988

Confidence is just one of the benefits that springs forth when we know who we are. We can refer back to ourselves, knowing that we have access to divine wisdom, and be comfortable with our choices and decisions. We don't have to rely on any outside sources for personal validation. *-Lissa Coffey*

> "All history makes clear that an indispensable quality
> of any man or class that wishes to lead, to hold power
> and privilege in society, is boundless self-confidence."
> -James Burnham (1905 - 1987)

Think of the word "confidence" and who comes to your mind? Chances are it is someone who is successful. Whether it is an athlete, a businessperson, or a rock star, confidence brings with it a kind of charisma. We can't help but notice! It seems the one thing successful people have in common, no matter what field they are in, is confidence. It radiates from them. *-Lissa Coffey*

> "With self-confidence fulfilled,
> You'll find that folk have confidence in you."
> -Goethe (1749-1832)

As an audience, we are attracted to confidence, because we would like to exude that ourselves! We have confidence in people who are self-confident. It shows strength, it shows fortitude and determination. But mostly, it shows an inner resolve that comes from knowing the true self. -*Lissa Coffey*

"Nothing so bolsters our self-confidence and reconciles
us with ourselves as the continuous ability to create;
to see things grow and develop under our hand,
day in, day out."
-Eric Hoffer (1902-1983)

We are creating our lives every day. When we see the fruits of our labor, we feel good about ourselves and our abilities. By attending to our spiritual practices every day, we are growing spiritually. We can be confident that we are on the path, and headed in the right direction. -*Lissa Coffey*

"If you think you can, you can. And if you think you
can't you're right."
-Mary Kay Ash (1985)

How many times do we sabotage ourselves from a lack of self-confidence? We are such powerful, creative people - and yet we doubt our own abilities! If we feel stuck, like we're not getting anywhere - we have to look carefully to see what is holding us back. And most of the times, the answer is ourselves. When we have confidence, we can soar! -*Lissa Coffey*

Connection

"Path presupposes distance;
If he be near, thou needest no path at all.
Verily, it makes one smile
To hear of a fish in water needing a drink."
-Kabir

We're all on this spiritual path, right? And where is it leading to? Back to our Selves! Somewhere on our journey we'll realize that we don't have to go anywhere or do anything to find God. God is not hiding from us! The Divine Presence is right here, where we are. Now and always. -*Lissa Coffey*

"I was always looking outside myself for strength
and confidence, but it comes from within.
It is there all the time."
-Anna Freud

We are wholly complete and capable human beings. Perhaps our greatest lesson in life is to understand this. We don't need to look outside ourselves for anything. All that we have, all that we are, is more than enough – it's perfect! -*Lissa Coffey*

"Ultimately there are no dualities – neither black nor
white, neither oppressor nor victim. We are all
connected in a journey toward the happiness that is
labeled enlightenment."
-His Holiness the Dalai Lama

There are no dualities, there is nothing outside ourselves. We are all One. Our connection to each other is reflective of our connection with God. There is no beginning, there is no end. It is ever-present and eternal. We are not alone in this life, ever. We are bound together, to learn and grow and help one another. It is our purpose, it is our privilege. -*Lissa Coffey*

"Nonbeing can never be;being can never not be.
Both these statements are obvious
To those who have seen the truth."
-The Bhagavad Gita

So, just where do we go to see "the truth?" If there were a cruise to get there I'll bet we'd all sign up! But we don't have to get on a luxury ship to see the Truth. We don't have to go anywhere. We just need to go within. It's all there. All the answers we seek. All the miracles we chase. Look within. You'll see. -*Lissa Coffey*

"We can only be said to be alive in those moments
when our hearts are conscious of our treasures."
-Thornton Wilder

A conscious heart: that's something to strive for! I have heard it said that the longest distance is the distance between the head and the heart. Why is this? Why do we not trust our hearts? We "think" we know better, but do we? We feel alive, energized, and happy when we feel love and gratitude. Our treasures are all around us and within us. We have only to open up our hearts to it, to open up our awareness to it. -*Lissa Coffey*

Conscience

"I should love to satisfy all, if I possibly can; but in trying
to satisfy all, I may be able to satisfy none. I have,
therefore, arrived at the conclusion that the best course
is to satisfy one's own conscience and leave the world to
form its own judgment, favorable or otherwise."
-Mohandas K. Gandhi (1869-1948)

I remember Jiminy Cricket singing "and always let your conscience be your guide." And I can still hear his little cricket voice from the Disney cartoon, I must have heard that dozens of times when I was a kid. I think the simple explanation I was given at that time was that your conscience would always tell you the right thing to do. If you listened to your conscience, you wouldn't give in to temptation and do something you would regret later. I may not have understood that completely when I was a child, but

I get it now. Sometimes it takes some life experience for us to really learn the lesson. Gandhi is saying here that you can't please everyone, so you've got to please yourself by doing what your conscience tells you is the best thing to do. Then basically let the chips fall where they may. *-Lissa Coffey*

"Let me consider this as a resolution by which I pledge myself to act in all variety of circumstances and to which I must recur often in times of carelessness and temptation - to measure my conduct by the rule of conscience."
-Ralph Waldo Emerson (1803-1882)

Just as conscience is a compass, it is also a measurement devise, according to Emerson. We really know how well we are doing, we don't need anyone's judgment or opinion of our behavior - we have our own conscience to mark our progress. There is nothing as freeing as a clear conscience. *-Lissa Coffey*

"Conscience itself asserts that it is a voice of God."
-Carl G. Jung (1875-1961)

"Conscience is God's presence in man."
-Emmanuel Swedenborg (1688-1772)

If conscience is that still small voice inside our heads, where does it come from? Who put it there? Our conscience is strong, and speaks to us loudly enough that we can't ignore it. It commands us to pay attention. *-Lissa Coffey*

"The needle of our conscience is as good a compass as any."
-Ruth Wolff, 1963

Our conscience tells us which way to go, it points us in the right direction, just as the needle of a compass does. Why would we purposely go astray with something so reliable helping us? This is something we can count on. *-Lissa Coffey*

"The one thing that doesn't abide by majority rule is a person's conscience."
-Harper Lee, To Kill a Mockingbird, 1960

A conscience is a very individual thing. We can't peak inside someone else's mind to find out just how they arrive at decisions. But we can look at our own thought process. "To Kill a Mockingbird" is a book that really explores the whole concept of conscience. I'm glad that my son will be reading it in school this year, we will have some great conversations about it. I can't help but picture Gregory Peck as Atticus. I love the way he portrayed this man who was so compelled to follow his conscience. I love the example that this character set for his children. *-Lissa Coffey*

Consistency

> "True consistency, that of the prudent and the wise, is to act in conformity with circumstances."
> -John C. Calhoun (1782-1850)

This is interesting to think about – so many times we look at consistency as a virtue. And it is in some situations. But when we look at the "big picture" we see how things change, and so why wouldn't our minds change with the times? For example, we might start out with an allegiance to a particular political party, only to change our minds and vote another way come election time. Is that being inconsistent? I don't think so. The consistency comes with being true to ourselves. *-Lissa Coffey*

> "A foolish consistency is the hobgoblin of little minds... Speak what you think now in hard words; and tomorrow speak what tomorrow thinks in hard words again, though it contradict everything you said today."
> -Ralph Waldo Emerson (1803-1882)

As we learn and grow we change our minds, we change our opinions, we open up our hearts to new possibilities. This is all good! Is it better to be "consistent" or to follow the truth of our hearts? I think politicians have a hard time because their opinions are so "on the record" that their past words often come back to haunt them. But we are each different people than we were five years ago, even five days ago or five minutes ago! Our hair changes, our style changes, and naturally, our feelings change, too. *-Lissa Coffey*

> "At the time of writing I never think of what I have said before. My aim is not to be consistent with my previous statements on a given question, but to be consistent with truth as it may present itself to me at the given moment. The result has been that I have grown from truth to truth."
> -Mohandas K. Gandhi (1869-1948)

The important thing to remember is that we are all doing the best we can with where we are and what we know so far. As time goes on, we learn more, and that might cause us to think differently. That is not to say that we were "wrong" before just because we have a different opinion now – but that we can make a more informed choice because of the experiences we have had in our lives. Things look different when they are viewed from a higher vantage point. *-Lissa Coffey*

> "Life hath its phases manifold,
> Yet still the new repeats the old;
> There is no truer truth than this:
> What was, is still the thing that is."
> -Julia C.R. Dorr, 1892

Nature presents such beautiful examples for us to learn from. Look at the changing over the seasons. Every day is different. And we go through extremes. And the seasons cycle and it seems like we're back where we started... except we're not! It's a new spring, or a new fall, and we're new right along with it. *-Lissa Coffey*

**"Consistency is contrary to nature, contrary to life.
The only completely consistent people are the dead."**
-Aldous Huxley

It is our nature to grow and to change. We evolve. We learn. Sometimes we shake things up with our new views and opinions – but that just promotes more growth. Sometimes we have to prune the dead branches from a tree in order for the new buds to have room to grow and for the tree to be healthy and thrive. We can prune away our outdated thinking, and leave room for expansion. *-Lissa Coffey*

Contentment

**"Happiness is neither virtue nor pleasure, nor this
thing nor that, but simply growth."**
-William Butler Yeats (1865-1939)

Contentment looks different to everyone. We may not be able to define it, or recognize it when we see it, but we can certainly feel it. Happiness and contentment spring from within. *-Lissa Coffey*

**"I have learned, in whatever state I am, to be content.
I know how to be abased, and I know how to abound;
in any and all circumstances I have learned the secret
of facing plenty and hunger, abundance and want."**
-Paul (A.D. 1st cent.)

When all around us is in flux, constantly moving and changing, can we keep our awareness on that still, calm, quiet within? That's where we find our peace. That's where we will find our contentment. *-Lissa Coffey*

**"Happiness is not achieved by the conscious pursuit of hap-
piness; it is generally the by-product of other activities."**
-Aldous Huxley (1894-1963)

If we substitute the word "money" for "happiness" in this quote it is easy to understand. Money is the by-product of industry and creativity. Money doesn't come to us by wishing for it, but by working for it. Happiness is also the result of our efforts and activities. It comes to us through our spiritual practices, our relationships, and our work. *-Lissa Coffey*

"The better part of happiness is to wish to be what you are."
-Desiderius Erasmus (1466-1536)

There's an old saying that "Happiness is not having what you want, but wanting what you have." When we know who we are, when we understand the truth of our greatness, we will know happiness because we will never wish to be anything other than ourselves. *-Lissa Coffey*

"Our happiness or unhappiness depends as much on our temperaments as on our luck."
-La Rochefoucauld (1613-1680)

Contentment is a choice. We have the choice in how we perceive our situations. We have the choice in how we react, and respond, to any circumstance. Circumstances change, and so can our temperament. Why not choose to look on the bright side? Let's try it, and see how it feels. Shift. *-Lissa Coffey*

Conversation

"Must we always talk for victory, and never once for truth, for comfort, and joy?"
-Ralph Waldo Emerson (1803-1882)

Conversation is a way for us to connect with people. And yet, how often do we feel like we need to impress someone, or demonstrate somehow that we have important opinions? If we could just drop that, and think more about connecting through Truth, about sharing ourselves rather than our "stuff" - then some meaningful conversation can take place. And we can experience that comfort and joy that leads to real friendship. *-Lissa Coffey*

"Speak not but what may benefit others or yourself; avoid trifling conversation."
-Benjamin Franklin (1706-1790)

Conversation. Communication between people. Conversation is often called an art, because it can take talent, and skill. We know when we've had a good conversation - we feel like there was an exchange of energy and ideas. We feel heard, and understood. We feel like we've learned something, or that we've spent our time well. It's more than just "small talk," it's something substantial - a meal rather than a snack! *-Lissa Coffey*

"The reason why we have two ears and only one mouth is that we may listen the more and talk the less."
-Zeno (335? - 263? B.C.)

In one of the acting classes I took years ago, one of the exercises was just to listen to another person speak. We paired up, one on one, and took turns telling a story. The point of the lesson was that acting is reacting. You can't just sit there and let the other person speak and at the same time be thinking about what you're going to say or do next. When we really listen, we react, we can't help it. Words move us, experiences affect us, people influence us. When we really listen we are open to all that, and that can be beautiful! It's natural, it's real. *-Lissa Coffey*

"The study of books is a languishing and feeble activity that gives no heat, whereas discussion teaches and exercises us at the same time."
-Montaigne (1533-1592)

Conversation is active. It's lively, it stretches our minds and imaginations! We are on this planet to learn from one another, and we do that by talking to each other, by conversing with each other! What good is reading books by the great philosophers, if you keep all this newfound wisdom and insight to yourself? It is meant to be shared, and discussed, and passed around the table for others to partake and add to the mix. *-Lissa Coffey*

"Silence is one of the great arts of conversation."
-Hannah More (1777)

One way we can tell that we are really close to someone, really comfortable with that person, is if we can just sit in silence together. So often we feel the need to fill those "awkward pauses" with idle chatter. But with some people, we're completely comfortable just sitting in silence. Sometimes more can be said in silence than can ever be said with words. *-Lissa Coffey*

Conviction

"Convictions are the mainsprings of action, the driving powers of life. What a man lives are his convictions."
-Bishop Francis Kelly

I love the word conviction because it is so strong and clear. It's more than a belief, it's a knowingness. There's no room for doubt. Our convictions move us forward. *-Lissa Coffey*

"The great thing in this world is not so much where we stand, as in what direction we are moving."
-Oliver Wendell Holmes

There's a zen saying that "wherever you go, there you are." Our convictions propel us to experience more of who we are. As we learn and grow, it may feel as if we're moving upward, outward, onward – but in reality we're moving inward, closer to our selves. *-Lissa Coffey*

"Soon after a hard decision something inevitably occurs to cast doubt. Holding steady against that doubt usually proves the decision."
-R.I. Fitzhenry

Our convictions are constantly challenged. That's just the nature of life. Even the foundation of the earth is challenged with floods and earthquakes, and yet it remains firm and steady. If we can hold up against the challenges and doubts, then it's confirmation to us that we are doing what is right for ourselves, and we can be at peace with that. *-Lissa Coffey*

"Conviction is worthless till it convert itself into Conduct."
-Thomas Carlyle (1795-1881)

Are we living the example? Do we say what we mean? Do we do what we say? Words are hollow unless we act on them. Our actions speak volumes, not only to those around us, but to ourselves. We need to be able to trust ourselves, to live in integrity, first and foremost. *-Lissa Coffey*

"There is a certain strong sense of inner conviction that strikes, with a pang as that of birth, through the very soul, and which is experienced but once or twice in a lifetime."
-E.M. Delafield, 1923

Sometimes we don't know why we know, but we know – we just KNOW. We recognize truth when we see it, for whatever reason. Maybe it's like "love at first sight," an instant recognition of a kindred spirit, or an epiphany that comes just when it's needed. We don't need to question, because in our heart we feel it. *-Lissa Coffey*

Courage

"Few persons have courage to appear as good as they really are."
-J.C. Hare (1795-1855) and A.W. Hare (1792-1834)

Is this so true? There is so much self-deprecation going on out there! Why do we fear our brilliance? Why do we hide our lights? We need to have the courage to shine! And we need to en-courage each other to bring it on - to share our gifts with the world, and with each other! *-Lissa Coffey*

"Courage charms us because it indicates that a man loves an idea better than all things in the world, that he is thinking neither of his bed, not his dinner, nor his money, but will venture all to put in act the invisible thought of his mind."
-Ralph Waldo Emerson (1803-1882)

Courage is attractive! What made Prince Charming so charming? His courage! The way that he fought dragons and witches and wouldn't let anything get in his way as he worked towards his goal. His goal was the most important thing to him - and his goal was love. It takes courage to love like that, with such abandon, with such totality. Who wouldn't be attracted to someone so courageous? *-Lissa Coffey*

"Courage: to bear unflinchingly what heaven sends."
-Euripides (485?-406 B.C.)

Courage is such a big word when we think about all that it means and all that it represents. There's the courage it takes to fight for what we believe in. There's the courage that we find when we need the strength to face adversity. We think of courage as being associated with heroes - and yet we all have the capacity to be courageous. We can all be heroes. *-Lissa Coffey*

"Fearlessness is the first requisite of spirituality."
-Mohandas K. Gandhi (1869-1948)

The Course in Miracles says that basically everything can be divided up into two choices, fear or love. And ultimately, it is all just love because fear is really just the absence of love. So, if fearlessness is courage, then courage is love. Courage is strength. It's the ability to call upon the strength and love that it inherent within each one of us, to bring it forth, to let it shine. *-Lissa Coffey*

"Life shrinks or expands in proportion to one's courage."
-Anais Nin (1903-1977)

The amount of courage that we have depends on the way that we see ourselves. Remember the Cowardly Lion in The Wizard of Oz? He went to see the Wizard because he did not like being cowardly - he wanted the Wizard to give him courage. And yet, just by setting out on the journey, taking that step forward into the unfamiliar, took a great deal of courage! And all along the way, the lion was put into situations where he could demonstrate his courage - and he did, without even realizing it! It takes until the end of the story for the lion to see that his courage was with him all the time. And with that discovery, his life expanded. *-Lissa Coffey*

Courtesy

"If a man be gracious and courteous to strangers, it shows he is a citizen of the world, and that his heart is no island cut off from other lands, but a continent that joins to them."
-Francis Bacon (1561-1626)

A citizen of the world. Yes! We are all in this together – no boundaries, no territories. We owe it to each other to show courtesy. In this way we are recognizing our heart connection. And our courtesy needs to extend to our friends and family, as well as strangers. Sometimes we take for granted that our family sits at the table with us and we don't think about our behavior. But it is so important to be kind and gracious both outside our homes and inside our homes. -*Lissa Coffey*

"The first point of courtesy must always be truth."
-Ralph Waldo Emerson (1803-1882)

I think the way I would change this quote just a little bit would be to write Truth with a capital "T." Truth, meaning that we present ourselves honestly and openly. Truth, meaning that we recognize the people in our lives as valuable and precious. Truth, meaning that we don't hide the light that shines within us, but that we share it with the world. -*Lissa Coffey*

"Life is not so short but that there is always time enough for courtesy."
-Ralph Waldo Emerson (1803-1882)

This is actually a very spiritual concept. Courtesy is more than just manners – it's kindness. It's showing both respect and appreciation for our fellow human beings. The way the world is today, being courteous can be a challenge at times. We get impatient, and frustrated, and short-tempered. But that's when it's time to take a breath and remember the wise words of Emerson, there is always time enough for courtesy. -*Lissa Coffey*

"The knock at the door tells the character of the visitor!"
-T.K.V. Desikachar, (Patanjali's Yogasutras: An introduction) 1987

Once again, a version of "actions speak louder than words." Interesting! How do we approach people? What is the first impression we give? I've seen a lot of courtesy go flying out the window with some e-mails! People are in a rush, they impulsively hit "send" and the ripples are felt throughout cyberland. Think about that "knock at the door" and how we can let others know that it is okay to let us in. -*Lissa Coffey*

"Good manners are the technique of expressing con- sideration for the feelings of others."
-Alice Duer Miller (1874-1942)

This is exactly what I've been teaching my boys ever since they were little. They're young men now, and sometimes they roll their eyes at me, but I know that this "training" will come in handy when they are out in the world. Doesn't it feel good to hold a door open for someone? Or to let someone go ahead of you in the supermarket? People seem so surprised at good manners sometimes, but it's such a simple gesture. Being kind and courteous helps make the world a better place! -*Lissa Coffey*

Creation

> **"Whenever man comes up with a better mousetrap,
> nature immediately comes up with a better mouse."**
> -James Carswell

We are constantly challenged. We're never quite "done." This is what keeps our creativity going. We'd get bored otherwise! It's hard to imagine what will be created in the future because things change so rapidly. But we do know that whatever comes up, we will create a solution, we will find a way. *-Lissa Coffey*

> **"Musical comedies aren't written, they are re-written."**
> -Stephen Sondheim

Many creative endeavors take sweat. It's a lot of work to get them to the point where we really feel that they are as good as they can be, the best that we can make them. The joy is in the process of creating. And when we feel we have reached completion, and created something that we can be proud of, the feeling is amazing. *-Lissa Coffey*

> **"I do not seek. I find."**
> -Pablo Picasso

When we've got our eyes open and we're wide awake we see that there is creativity all around us. And more importantly, we know that there is creativity within us. We can draw upon that creativity anytime we want to. We can use it to problem-solve, to brainstorm, to learn and to grow. *-Lissa Coffey*

> **"I am a choreographer. A choreographer is a poet.
> I do not create. God creates. I assemble, and I will
> steal from everywhere to do it."**
> -George Balanchine

We have so many tools to work with when we create, and one of them is our intelligence. We get an idea, and that is the spark that sends our creativity into play. We figure out how to get something done, how we can make something better, more efficient, more productive, or more beautiful. *-Lissa Coffey*

> **"In creating, the only hard thing's to begin;
> A grass-blade's no easier to make than an oak."**
> -James Russell Lowell

We are creative beings. Some people might argue that they're not creative, saying that they don't paint or write or cook. But creation is not just about art. We are creating our lives every single day. We create relationships, we create work, we create and invent and expand because that is our nature. *-Lissa Coffey*

Creativity

"Any creative endeavor is channeled, whether it be music
or art or theoretical science. We have the capacity to tune in
to energies and to convert them into reality for ourselves."
-Frank Alper

At one important scientific conference, a group of scientists announced that with all of the new technology and their vast knowledge, that they could create life all on their own, with no help whatsoever from God. A reporter in the room challenged them and asked for proof. The scientists, confident in their claim, invited everyone outside for a demonstration. There, in an open field, one of them scooped a handful of earth, and said: "This is where we will begin." And God's voice was heard from above and He said: "Use your own dirt!"

This is a cute joke, and it calls our attention to the fact that we are creative beings, and that creativity comes from the Source of All things. -*Lissa Coffey*

"To fulfill a dream, to be allowed to sweat over lonely
labor, to be given the chance to create, is the meat and
potatoes of life. The money is the gravy. As everyone
else, I love to dunk my crust in it. But alone, it is not a
diet designed to keep body and soul together."
-Bette Davis

Our creativity is our nourishment, it is nutrition for our spirit! We cannot truly live without it. We are born creative beings, and we are creating every moment with every decision that we make. We are creating our lives right now. -*Lissa Coffey*

"When we are writing, or painting, or composing, we
are, during the time of creativity, freed from normal
restrictions, and are opened to a wider world, where
colors are brighter, sounds clearer, and people more
wondrously complex than we normally realize."
-Madeleine L'Engle, (Walking on Water 1980)

Creativity is freeing. It is exploring the great "what if" out there. When our imagination is unleashed we can soar to ever-greater heights. We experience our connection to the Universe in a profound way, with timeless awareness and innate wisdom.
-*Lissa Coffey*

"We were born to make manifest the glory of God
within us."
-Nelson Mandela

Part of our purpose in life lies in our creativity. We are each an individual expression of God, and we each have a special contribution to bring to this planet. What makes your heart sing? What do you love to do? When you are doing that, you are expressing the divine presence within you. It's joyful, it's glorious! -*Lissa Coffey*

"Creativity can be described as letting go of certainties."
-Gail Sheehy, (Pathfinders, 1981)

What is certain anyway? If anything, certainty is habit, and it can get boring! It's time to break the mold, shake things up, create a new paradigm! There are infinite possibilities out there, and within each one of us... let's start trying them on for size!
-Lissa Coffey

Decisions

"Living is a constant process of deciding what we are
going to do."
-José Ortega y Gasset

Every moment we're making decisions. Some decisions are small and some are big, but they all lead us to right where we are. If past decisions have led us to this place, it follows that future decisions will lead us further down the road. So, where do we want to go? Think about it and then decide! *-Lissa Coffey*

"Choice of attention – is to the inner life what choice
of action is to the outer. In both cases, a man is
responsible for his choice and must accept the
consequences, whatever they may be."
-W.H. Auden

We decide where we put our attention, and wherever we put our attention grows, and becomes more important in our lives. We decide how to spend our days, what to read, where to go, what to say and with whom to talk. All of that has some affect on our inner life. We can feel it; we can see the results. *-Lissa Coffey*

"The percentage of mistakes in quick decisions is no
greater than in long-drawn-out vacillations, and the
effect of decisiveness itself "makes things go" and
creates confidence."
-Anne O'Hare McCormick

There's a lot to be said for making decisions quickly. When we go with our gut, follow our instincts, our decisions usually turn out to be good ones. But sometimes if we think too much, or over-analyze the situation, we just confuse ourselves. A quick decision saves time and energy. *-Lissa Coffey*

"I would sort out all the arguments and see which
belonged to fear and which to creativeness.
Other things being equal, I would make the
decision which had the larger number of
creative reasons on its side."
-Katharine Butler Hathaway

A lot of people know the strategy of making a list of "pros" and "cons" when making a decision – but this helps us to sort things out a little differently, a little more creatively. Fear tends to make us fall into indecision, or no decision. Creativity may involve risk, and change, and it can move us towards action and progress. *-Lissa Coffey*

"Decision is a sharp knife that cuts clean and straight; indecision, a dull one that hacks and tears and leaves ragged edges behind it."
-Gordon Graham

In a state of indecision we can't move – we're stuck, stagnant. Indecision weighs us down. Indecision hurts us by wasting our time, and the time of everyone around us who is affected by the indecision. But decision, even if it's a tough decision, moves us forward. We are clear and concise and those around us know where we stand so that they can make their own decisions with more knowledge of the overall situation. *-Lissa Coffey*

Desire

"Desire is the very essence of man."
- Benedict De Spinoza, Ethics

Interesting word, "desire." It evokes a lot of feeling. No wonder so many pop songs use it to describe a heart's yearning... can't you just hear the Backstreet Boys now? "You are my fire, my one desire!" Desire is man's great motivator, it spurs us into action! Through action comes experience, achievement, accomplishment, and many great things.

So, you have a desire... now what do you do with it? Of course, you want to fulfill it! We are busy fulfilling our desires everyday, and sometimes so easily that we aren't even aware of what we are doing. Let's look at the mechanics of desire fulfillment:

1. Recognize the desire.
2. Evaluate the desire - do you REALLY want it?
3. Create an intention to fulfill the desire.
4. Release the desire to the universe - state your intention clearly.
5. Give up any attachment to the outcome... anything can happen, and it's usually better than we ever could have anticipated.
6. Let the universe handle the details - don't try to control or manipulate how things happen.
7. Express gratitude!

-Lissa Coffey

"Heaven always favors good desires."
-Cervantes (Don Quixote)

What makes a "good" desire? All of our desires are good! We have our desires for a reason, and we wouldn't have them if we were not capable of fulfilling them. Be like Don Quixote, and "follow that star!" Our desires lead us to our destiny. *-Lissa Coffey*

**"Our desires always increase with our possessions;
the knowledge that something remains yet unenjoyed,
impairs our enjoyment of the good before us."**
-Samuel Johnson

As we continue on the spiritual path, we notice that our desires change. While we recognize that desire for material things is our human nature, the novelty of those things subsides. We yearn to experience our connection with God more fully. Our desire for spiritual growth moves us along the path. -*Lissa Coffey*

**"Desires are the pulses of the soul; as physicians judge
by the appetite, so may you by desires."**
-Thomas Manton

Our desires tell us a lot about ourselves. Ask yourself today: "What do I want?" Look at that carefully and ask again: "What do I REALLY want?" Then look at that and ask: "Why do I want that?" Oftentimes that question will get you to the true answer of what you REALLY want! And how would you change your life if you had that? What would be different? Can you do that now? Play "what if" a little and see if you can get yourself closer to your goals right now. -*Lissa Coffey*

Destiny

**"Destiny is not a matter of chance, it is a matter of
choice; it is not a thing to be waited for, it is a thing to
be achieved."**
-William Jennings Bryan (1860-1925)

This is one of the big spiritual discussions of all time - how much of our life is pre-determined by destiny versus how much control or how much say we have in what happens to us in this life. No matter what happens outside of us, we still have the choice in how we respond to it. That choice is what allows us to create our own future. -*Lissa Coffey*

"It is not in the stars to hold our destiny but in ourselves."
-William Shakespeare

We each are here for a reason. Sometimes we know the reason, sometimes we don't, it is up to each one of us to find that reason for ourselves. Sometimes we just have to go along, doing our stuff, knowing that when we follow our hearts it leads us to where we need to be. And wherever that is, is not only for our own good, but for the collective good. We learn from each other, and somehow, everything works out. -*Lissa Coffey*

"I am not afraid... I was born to do this."
-Joan of Arc (1429)

"All I was doing was trying to get home from work."
-Rosa Parks, on refusing to move to the back of the bus, televised interview (1985)

I had to put these two quotes together because both of these two women showed such courage. They both saw the "big picture" and understood their role in it. Although these events happened centuries apart, one could say that they were destined. Things could not have continued the way that they were going, and each of these women had a part in changing things. They could have backed down or shied away from it - but instead they chose to step up and be where they were, where they felt they were "supposed" to be. *-Lissa Coffey*

"Destiny's bank is inexorable, all accounts must balance."
-Dorothy Fuldheim, A Thousand Friends (1974)

How do accounts balance? It's simple - what you put into it you get out of it. It's just like the law of cause and effect. It's a principle of nature - and that's just the way it is. In Eastern philosophy, the accounts may not necessarily balance in one lifetime, but over many lifetimes. It's looking at that big picture again. Life may not seem "fair" at one particular time - but it generally is when you look back over the long run. *-Lissa Coffey*

"Death and life have their determined appointments;
riches and honors depend upon heaven."
-Confucius (550-478 B.C.)

To me this says that we are here on this earth at this particular time for a reason. We have kept our appointment. What we do with the time we have here is up to us. The rewards are not necessarily material, but much more valuable- our spiritual growth, the love and fulfillment we find and create for ourselves. We have choices in how we spend our time, and the lessons we learn along the way are our bounty. *-Lissa Coffey*

Discovery

"Of all the discoveries which men need to make, the
most important, at the present moment, is that of the
self-forming power treasured up in themselves."
-William Ellery Channing (1780-1842)

The word brings discovery to mind images of Christopher Columbus and Thomas Edison. Life is such a great frontier, with so many treasures "our there" for us to find. We can soar into space, we can break down DNA. And now, as always, we need to look within, to discover the wisdom and the power which is an inherent part of our being. *-Lissa Coffey*

> **"Very often if happens that a discovery is made whilst working upon quite another problem."**
> -Thomas Alva Edison (1847-1931)

Sometimes if we are focused too intensely on a problem, we get caught up in it and can't see the forest for the trees. This is when it is time to detach, to turn our attention to something else and let our minds do some re-shuffling without our stubborn influence. And then, sure enough, we get that "ah-ha!" moment, and a discovery is made!
-Lissa Coffey

> **"The intellect has little to do on the road to discovery. There comes a leap in consciousness, call it intuition or what you will, and the solution comes to you and you don't know how or why."**
> -Albert Einstein (1879-1955)

Albert Einstein knew that there was a purpose for time spent in quiet. In silence we have access to all the wisdom of the universe. We don't have to reach for it, the wisdom comes to us when we are open to it, and allow it space to come in. We can soak it up, marinate in it! And then, lo and behold, the wisdom is there for us when we need it.
-Lissa Coffey

> **"The secret of all those who make discoveries is that they regard nothing as impossible."**
> -Justus Leibig (1803-1973)

When we are open to infinite possibilities we know that there is a solution to every problem, an answer to every question. It might take investigation, and experimentation, determination and a lot of faith – but with this mind-set, a discovery will be made. *-Lissa Coffey*

> **"Most new discoveries are suddenly-seen things that were always there."**
> -Susanne K. Langer, 1942

Whenever an explorer "discovered" a new land it wasn't as if it just popped up in front of him or her. It was there, always, perhaps even waiting to be found and utilized. If we go down the same road everyday, we tend to become familiar with our surroundings, and after awhile we don't bother to look anymore. And one day something catches our eye and we think: "wow, when did that change?" We don't need to travel to exotic locales to learn new things. It's amazing what we can discover right where we are. *-Lissa Coffey*

Dreams

"Within each one of us there is another whom we do
not know. He speaks to us in dreams and tells us how
differently he sees us from how we see ourselves.
When, therefore, we find ourselves in a difficult situation,
to which there is no solution, he can sometimes kindle
a light that radically alters our attitude, the very attitude
that led us into the difficult situation."
-Carl G. Jung (1875-1961)

This "another whom we do not know" is indeed our Higher Self, or God, or Spirit, or whatever we each may want to call that Divine energy within. Yet as we work on our spiritual growth, the point is to get to know this "another" and by doing so to understand that there really is no separation between us! We come to realize who we really are. -*Lissa Coffey*

"The interpretation of dreams is the royal road to a
knowledge of the unconscious activities of the mind."
-Sigmund Freud (1856-1939)

We can look at our dreams, and learn from them. And what we learn is more about ourselves! This is just another way that God speaks to us – it is just another opportunity for us to grow. And it's all open to interpretation, just like life. What do we see, what do we feel, what do we experience? It is different for each of us – and isn't that great? -*Lissa Coffey*

All that we see or seem
Is but a dream within a dream."
-Edgar Allan Poe (1809-1845)

What is real? It has been said that the first three states of consciousness (sleeping, dreaming and waking) are just an illusion. That "reality" comes with higher states of consciousness, when we can see God in all things, and when we can see the Oneness of all creation. When we "wake up" to reality, we will see the beauty of life all around us at all times. -*Lissa Coffey*

"I've dreamt in my life dreams that have stayed with
me ever after, and changed my ideas: they've gone
through and through me, like wine through water, and
altered the color of my mind."
-Emily Bronte, Wuthering Heights (1847)

Whether we're talking about dreams that occur in our sleep state, or dreams as ambitions, we have these experiences for a reason. Dreams become a part of us, a part of who we are, and a factor in the decisions that we make. Embrace your dreams, pursue them, and watch them change and grow as you do. -*Lissa Coffey*

"When you dream, you dialogue with aspects of yourself that normally are not with you in the daytime and
you discover that you know a great deal more than you
thought you did."
-Toni Cade Bambara, in Sturdy Black Bridges (1979)

Dreams are a place where we can figure things out about ourselves. They help us to see what motivates us, what our true desires are, and where we are headed. They help us to become more of who we really are! *-Lissa Coffey*

Earth

"Old Earth, worn by the ages, wracked by rain and storm, exhausted yet ever ready to produce what life must have to go on!"
-Charles de Gaulle (1890-1970)

Earth is the ground under our feet, our base, our stability. The earth is solid, reliable, sound. And it is also forgiving, and loving. We can do our part by loving the earth back, and treating it with the care and kind attention that it deserves. *-Lissa Coffey*

"The most important fact about Spaceship Earth: An instruction book didn't come with it."
-R. Buckminster Fuller (1895-1983)

This beautiful blue planet of ours seems like a sports car fresh off the dealership floor. But sports cars, and spaceships, are lifeless. They only move when we put in the gas and push the pedal. The Earth is a living, vital, organism. Rather than taking care of it as we would a car, giving it a wash and an oil change every once in awhile, we need to treat it more like a person. Every living creature has needs – and since Earth provides for our needs, we need to provide for the Earth's needs. *-Lissa Coffey*

"Our earthly ball a peopled garden."
-Goethe (1749-1832)

What grows springs from the earth. We are a part of it all! Like the plants, trees, flowers, and animal life – we are living and growing amongst it all. How are we contributing to the beauty of this garden? Whether it is with our work, or our art, or our kindness, we have opportunities daily to bring glory to this planet. *-Lissa Coffey*

"What is the use of a house if you haven't got a tolerable planet to put it on?"
-Henry David Thoreau (1817-1862)

The earth is our home. Home sweet home! We need to give it love, to give it attention. When our house gets run down we fix it up, do some spring cleaning, add a fresh coat of paint. The earth needs the same kind of care. Keeping our waters clean, and our skies clear – all of that is our responsibility. We can start right where we are.
-Lissa Coffey

"In this broad earth of ours,
Amid the measureless grossness and the slag,
Enclosed and safe within its central heart,
Nestles the seed perfection."
-Walt Whitman (1819-1892)

There is an underlying perfection to this world. Sometimes we can't see it with all the problems and pollution, but it is there anyway. When we hold that truth in our consciousness, and focus on that perfection, we can bring it into the light. Think peace.
-Lissa Coffey

Effort

"John Wooden taught us that doing the best you are
capable of is victory enough."
-Kareem Abdul-Jabbar

John Wooden, who coached UCLA's championship basketball team for so many years, was and still is one of the best-loved sports figures out there. He is an icon, a legend. What made him such a great coach was not only his love of the game, but his love of his players, and his love of life. John Wooden was a philosopher. He was a sage. We would all do well to listen to what he had to say! *-Lissa Coffey*

"Satisfaction lies in the effort, not in the attainment.
Full effort is full victory."
-Mohandas K. Gandhi (1869-1948)

Full effort is mindfulness. It's being present in the moment, concentrating on the task at hand and not on the results. When we're in that space where we're putting in effort, doing our best, we lose track of time and experience the now. That's a victory!
-Lissa Coffey

"You can't always get what you want.
But if you try sometimes,
You just might find
You get what you need."
-Mick Jagger and Keith Richards song, 1969

It usually takes something to motivate us to make that effort. It's like we begin with the end in mind – that's our goal, what we are working towards. But along the way, things might change. We certainly change and grow from the experience – and maybe that's just what we really need. We can find some of the most amazing spiritual messages in our own music. Are we listening? *-Lissa Coffey*

"I know of no more encouraging fact than the
unquestionable ability of man to elevate his life
by a conscious endeavor."
-Henry David Thoreau (1817-1862)

Yes! This is totally encouraging! In the choices that we make, we have the ability to change, and improve our lives! Where are we choosing to put our efforts? What endeavors have we chosen to pursue? I found another quote said: "Rowing harder doesn't help if the boat is headed in the wrong direction." (Kenichi Ohmae, 1989) If we happen to re-evaluate and decide that this particular endeavor has not rewarded our efforts in some way, we can choose again, change direction! And we take with us our experiences and newfound knowledge. *-Lissa Coffey*

> "Babies are a nuisance, of course. But so does every-
> thing seem to be that is worth while – husbands and
> books and committees and being loved and everything.
> We have to choose between barren ease and rich unrest."
> -Winifred Holtby, in Vera Brittain, Testament of Friendship, 1940

Everything worthwhile involves effort. And it's true that we get out of life what we put into it. Put in nothing, get back nothing. Put in some effort and love and reap the rewards! If we want a rich life, spiritually and otherwise, we've got to go for it! Doing our practices, whether it is prayer, meditation, volunteer work, reading, or anything – takes effort, takes time. But we feel the good at work in our lives. We see things from a different perspective. We know we are growing and learning and it is all so worth it! *-Lissa Coffey*

Emotion

> "It is the emotion which drives the intelligence for-
> ward in spite of obstacles."
> -Henri Bergson (1859-1941)

It has been said that necessity is the mother of invention. But what creates the necessity? Some human emotion that cries out for attention. And then to satisfy that need, our intelligence kicks into high gear. When we want something really badly, we somehow figure out a way to get it. *-Lissa Coffey*

> "Emotion is the moment when steel meets flint and a
> spark is struck forth, for emotion is the chief source of
> consciousness. There is no change from darkness to
> light or from inertia to movement without emotion."
> -Carl G. Jung (1875-1961)

What would life be like without emotion? I would think it would be rather dull and boring. One way we judge a good movie is if it engages our emotions. Do we care about the characters? Are we caught up in the action? Life is like that, too. We remember moments by the emotions we feel at the time. The joy of holding a newborn baby. The despair over the loss of a loved one. The feeling of accomplishment after running a marathon. These emotions show us that we are alive. *-Lissa Coffey*

"Emotion: The human spirit experienced in the flesh."
-Jerry Tucker

When we "wear our heart on our sleeve" it means that we show our emotion. Emotions can be positive or negative, but they certainly are an important part of our existence. Emotions are one thing that makes us human – we are here with these bodies to feel all these feelings and learn and grow from the experience. *-Lissa Coffey*

"Ninety percent of our lives is governed by emotion. Our brains merely register and act upon what is telegraphed to them by our bodily experience. Intellect is to emotion as our clothes are to our bodies: we could not very well have civilized life without clothes, but we would be in a poor way if we had only clothes without bodies."
-Alfred North Whitehead (1861-1947)

We need both heart and head to function in this world. And we function best when they are working in tandem. There is a reason why we are wired this way, and we figure it out when we try to use one too much without the other. *-Lissa Coffey*

"Those who don't know how to weep with their whole heart don't know how to laugh either."
-Golda Meir, 1973

Emotions are meant to be expressed. We can't bottle them up inside or we will do damage to ourselves. Of course, we need to express our emotions in a healthy way – no going off throwing chairs as a way to express anger! And as we mature spiritually we are more and more comfortable with expressing our emotions in appropriate and positive ways. *-Lissa Coffey*

Empowerment

"It's not enough to just swing at the ball. You've got to loosen your girdle and really let it fly."
-Babe Didrikson Zaharias

Empowerment. What a great word. This is power that we create, within ourselves, for ourselves. Babe Didrikson Zaharias was one of the best female golfers in history. She knew how it felt to be empowered and it showed in her confidence. It showed in her swing! *-Lissa Coffey*

"'How does one become a butterfly?' she asked pensively. 'You must want to fly so much that you are willing to give up being a caterpillar.'"
-Trina Paulus

Empowerment means going beyond our comfort zone. It's reaching within to find what it takes to move us beyond where we are to where we want to be. We have that power, but whether it lies dormant or it is put into action is completely up to us. *-Lissa Coffey*

"True genius doesn't fulfill expectations, it shatters them."
-Arlene Croce

I think of Buzz Lightyear, the astronaut in the movie Toy Story when he says: "To infinity, and beyond!" That's empowerment – no limits, just potential. Whatever we can dream, we can achieve. *-Lissa Coffey*

"In my experience, there is only one motivation, and that is desire. No reasons or principle contain it or stand against it."
-Jane Smiley

Desire moves us to action. The bigger the desire, the swifter the action. When we really want something, we get creative, and pull out all the stops. We engage our intelligence, we find the means to fulfill our desire. We become empowered. *-Lissa Coffey*

"When one paints an ideal, one does not need to limit one's imagination."
-Ellen Key

In the film world, we see that anything is possible. Why? Because there are writers and actors and directors working together to create a reality for the big screen. Many of these production companies have names that emphasize that it is an illusion that we are watching, like "Dreamworks" or "Imagine Films." In the "real" world, anything is possible, but we don't always believe it. We limit ourselves to what we have already experienced, or what we can see, or feel. But the truth is that we are creating our reality everyday, just the same way that filmmakers are making movies. We're writing our script, and acting it out. If we want to change something, we can change it. We have that power. *-Lissa Coffey*

Energy

"Energy is Eternal Delight."
-William Blake (1757-1827)

Think about the energy of the sun. It provides light and heat and even solar power. It is there for us all day; we can count on it. And through the great organizational power of the universe, night falls. Day and night. Activity and silence. There is a lesson for us here. Delight in the differences. Energy gained through silence can be joyful, fruitful, and enriching. *-Lissa Coffey*

> **"The worshipper of energy is too physically energetic
> to see that he cannot explore certain higher fields
> until he is still."**
> -Clarence Day (1874-1935)

Since I have been teaching meditation, many people have said to me: "I can't meditate, I have too much energy!" Energy can be our ally, it gives us the vitality we need to accomplish, to excel. And yet, if we can't tame our energy enough to allow ourselves to sit still and just be, then that energy can be counterproductive. Yes, energy is good! And we can make much better use of it when we spend some time in silence. -*Lissa Coffey*

> **"The greater the tension, the greater is the potential.
> Great energy springs from a correspondingly great
> tension of opposites."**
> -Carl G. Jung (1875-1961)

It's all about balance. If we are in that "go go go" mode all the time then we burn ourselves out. We need time for silence, we need time to recharge our batteries. Then we can come at life from a new, fresh perspective. -*Lissa Coffey*

> **"Life engenders life. Energy creates energy. It is by
> spending oneself that one becomes rich."**
> -Sarah Bernhardt (1966)

Energy is one of those things that seems to be contagious! Have you ever noticed how a low-energy meeting gets revved up when someone comes up with a great idea? We feed off each others' energy all the time! How great is it to be the one who can light up a room?! Let's do what we can to lift the energy around us every day – it could be as simple as sharing a smile. -*Lissa Coffey*

> **"Energy is the power that drives every human being.
> It is not lost by exertion but maintained by it,
> for it is a faculty of the psyche."**
> -Germaine Greer (1973)

Sometimes when we're feeling down or tired, the best thing to pick us up is a brisk walk! A little exertion of energy gets the juices flowing – then we can think more clearly and make better decisions for ourselves. We need to strive for a balance between quiet and activity. Too much of either one gets us out of kilter. -*Lissa Coffey*

Enjoyment

> **"Enjoyment is not a goal, it is a feeling that accompanies
> important ongoing activity."**
> -Paul Goodman

If we're doing what we love, then we're not really working at all. "Work" can be enjoyable. Look at all the joy we can get out of one day, from enjoying our homes, our meals, our family and friends, and our time spent in nature. This is important activity. *-Lissa Coffey*

**"Enthusiasm is the greatest asset in the world.
It beats money and power and influence."**
-Henry Chester

One of my favorite quotes ever is from Ralph Waldo Emerson who said: "Nothing great was ever achieved without enthusiasm." Enthusiasm can take us very far. Enthusiasm is the expression of that joy of life, of living, of participating, of just being. There's a reason why people say that enthusiasm is contagious – it is! We respond to it, and can't help but feel it ourselves. *-Lissa Coffey*

"The man is richest whose pleasures are the cheapest."
-Henry David Thoreau

A walk in the park. A child's laughter. A hug from a friend. The first blooms in spring. What brings a smile to your face? Life is filled with things to enjoy. It's up to us to find them, and enjoy them. *-Lissa Coffey*

"All the great pleasures in life are silent."
-Georges Clemenceau

What is the sound of love, joy, or beauty? These are things we recognize because we feel them, we know them. Great composers have tried to express this with music, and great poets have tried to put it into words. And yet love and joy and beauty are too big to be captured on any canvas, or any recording. We can close our eyes, we can listen to the silence, and find them anytime. *-Lissa Coffey*

**"We act as though comfort and luxury were the chief
requirements of life, when all that we need to make us
really happy is something to be enthusiastic about."**
-Charles Kingsley

Think about little kids at play; when they're having fun the enthusiasm shows on their faces. They look happy. It doesn't matter if it's raining or they have the latest, greatest toys, they're living in the moment, totally present to what is going on. We can be like that. We can enjoy ourselves, it's a choice we make. *-Lissa Coffey*

Enthusiasm

> "Nothing is so contagious as enthusiasm; it moves stones,
> it charms brutes. Enthusiasm is the genius of sincerity,
> and truth accomplishes no victories without it."
> -Edward Bulwer-Lytton

Enthusiasm is really spirit bubbling through us, that's why it's so contagious! It is attractive, magnetic even – people around can't help but get a lift from all that positive energy emanating forth. Enthusiasm feels good. It is real, and natural, and life affirming. *-Lissa Coffey*

> "All we need to make us really happy is something to
> be enthusiastic about."
> -Charles Kingsley

There are so many things that we could be enthusiastic about, but do we let ourselves get worked up? Too often we hold back, we say we don't want to "get our hopes up" or we're afraid to jump into something when we might fall back on our behinds. But there's a reason why we get enthusiastic about the things that we get enthusiastic about – and that's to lead us toward happiness! Enthusiasm is a cue for us to participate, get involved, "just do it!" *-Lissa Coffey*

> "Flaming enthusiasm, backed up by horse sense and
> persistence, is the quality that most frequently makes
> for success."
> -Dale Carnegie

Remember that formula! When we're really excited about something, if we want to make something happen, all we need to do is to share our enthusiasm, use common sense, and don't give up! It's that simple. Success begins with enthusiasm.
-Lissa Coffey

> "The measure of an enthusiasm must be taken between
> interesting events. It is between bites that the luke-
> warm angler loses heart."
> -Edwin Way Teale

Can't you just picture this scenario? A fisherman who LOVES to fish doesn't just love those moments when he actually lands one – he loves the whole process. Similarly, an actor with an enthusiasm for his craft is just as happy doing a part in a community theatre play as he would be starring in a feature film. What makes for an "interesting event?" What compels us to hang in there? It's the whole process that generates enthusiasm when we truly love to do what we do. *-Lissa Coffey*

> "No one keeps up his enthusiasm automatically.
> Enthusiasm must be nourished with new actions, new
> aspirations, new efforts, new vision. Compete with
> yourself; set your teeth and dive into the job of
> breaking your own record. It is one's own fault
> if his enthusiasm is gone; he has failed to feed it."
> -Papyrus

Knowing that enthusiasm fuels our fire and keeps us going, it is up to us to maintain the enthusiasm necessary to keep ourselves on track. Enthusiasm can be found, and it can be created. So if you can't find it, make it! *-Lissa Coffey*

Environment

> "I believe natural beauty has a necessary place in the
> spiritual development of any individual or any society.
> I believe that whenever we destroy beauty, or whenever
> we substitute something man-made and artificial for
> a natural feature of the earth, we have retarded some
> part of man's spiritual growth."
> -Rachel Carson (1907-1964)

When we talk about the oneness of the universe - we're not just talking about people. We live with and amongst nature. We share this planet with everything that is here. We're all made up of the same "stuff." We need nature and it's nutrients to nourish ourselves! Nature nourishes our bodies, and it also nurtures our spirit. The profound peace that we feel when we are in the mountains, or under a starry sky, is food for our soul. *-Lissa Coffey*

> "In the relations of man with the animals, with the
> flowers, with the objects of creation, there is a great
> ethic, scarcely perceived as yet, which will at length
> break forth into light."
> -Victor Hugo (1802-1885)

Victor Hugo said this over 100 years ago. Do you think that the ethic has broken forth into light? What will it take for the world to understand that we are intricately connected to our environment? There are people and organizations making great efforts to preserve our environment, and to stop a lot of the abuse of nature that has been going on. But it seems like these organizations have to fight to get their message across. Hopefully with the growing popularity of hybrid cars, and solar power, we'll be able to make a difference - and show that we are evolving, technologically and spiritually. *-Lissa Coffey*

> "I am I plus my surroundings; and if I do not preserve
> the latter, I do not preserve myself."
> -Jose Ortega y Gasset (1883-1955)

I know that this spiritual community totally understands the meaning of these words. When we get into that space where we can't tell where we leave off and the environment begins, it is total bliss. We know that taking care of the environment is the same thing as taking care of ourselves. -*Lissa Coffey*

> "There is a unity of the body with the environment,
> as well as a unity of the body and soul into one person."
> -Alfred North Whitehead (1861-1947)

When my kids were little they watched "The Lion King" on video over and over again. They loved the animals, they could relate to them - and they totally "got" the whole Circle of Life message. I think this new generation is more sensitive about the environment, maybe because they grew up with more of an awareness of it. There are recycling bins in every home now, so kids are getting into better habits at a younger age. -*Lissa Coffey*

> "I had assumed that the Earth, the spirit of the Earth,
> noticed exceptions - those who wantonly damage it and
> those who do not. But the Earth is wise. It has given itself
> into the keeping of all, and all are therefore accountable."
> -Alice Walker, 1988

That really is the way it works, isn't it? The Earth can't differentiate one person from another, because we're all one! So, what one of us does affects all of us. We're all in this together; we can't afford to be selfish. We have to keep the "big picture" in mind at all times. -*Lissa Coffey*

Eternity

> "Eternity is not something that begins after you are
> dead. It is going on all the time. We are in it now."
> -Charlotte Perkins Gilman, 1909

I can't help but think about the movie titled "From Here to Eternity," a classic love story. When we start "here" and go "to" eternity, we're reaching into the boundless future. But really, eternity is the infinite past and the future as well. There is no beginning, there is no end. There is no time, there is no space. And yet somehow we've carved out this little slice of life, where we exist here and now: the present. Where do we go from here? Ah – the sweet mysteries that lie ahead! -*Lissa Coffey*

> "What, to eternity, is a thousand years? Not so much
> as the blinking of an eye to the turning of the slowest
> of the spheres."
> Dante (A.D. 1265 - 1321)

A thousand years. Think of all the things that happen in what seems like this large amount of time. The changes that take place, the leaps and bounds made in progress, the contributions made by the people who lived during that time. And yet, some history books can sum up a century in a chapter of two! The more we move through time the more we have to write about. History may "repeat itself," but we have something to learn from it each time. As we rack up the centuries, we have to wonder what the world will look like in a few more "blinks of an eye." -*Lissa Coffey*

"The eternity of the moment."
-Hermann Hesse (1877-1962)

The beauty of the moment. It all comes down to that really. We can't predict the future, it can change with a thought. We can't change the past, what's done is done. But we can live in, and enjoy, and appreciate this precious present moment. When we are totally in the moment, time stands still. -*Lissa Coffey*

"The things that are unseen are eternal."
-Paul (A.D. 1st cent.)

What is unseen? Some of the things that are unseen are felt, and that's how we understand their presence. Love, joy, truth, wisdom. These things are precious, and timeless. What Paul said back in the first century is as wise and true then as it is now, and as it will be centuries from now. The love that we feel, and express, will live on always. Love never dies, love is eternal. -*Lissa Coffey*

"The clock indicates the moment - but what does eternity indicate?"
-Walt Whitman (1819-1892)

I like these thought-provoking questions! A clock is merely a form of measurement. Time marches on. We check days off our calendars one by one – done, complete, something else accomplished. But eternity, wow – vast, huge, unlimited potential, beyond any time we could possibly comprehend. Something way bigger than ourselves. And maybe that's the answer – eternity represents infinite possibilities. Anything can happen! So why not dream, and plan, and create a wonderful future for ourselves? -*Lissa Coffey*

Evolution

"I am not a thing, a noun. I seem to be a verb, an evolutionary process – an integral function of the universe."
-R. Buckminster Fuller (1895-1983)

We are growing, we are learning, we are evolving – every minute, every day! This is an active process – an ongoing process. It is part of what makes us who we are, it is a part of the beauty of being human. -*Lissa Coffey*

> "I think it not improbable that man, like the grub that prepares a chamber for the winged thing it never has seen but is to be – that man may have cosmic destinies that he does not understand. And so beyond the vision of battling races and an impoverished earth, I catch a dreaming glimpse of peace."
> -Oliver Wendell Holmes, Jr. (1841-1935)

If we all hold to that vision of peace, of compassion, of goodness – we, as a society and as a world, will evolve towards that vision. Like the caterpillar that was born to evolve into a butterfly – we have a purpose which lies beyond our daily scope of events. There is so much more to us than we can see. And so much that we can contribute than we can comprehend. *-Lissa Coffey*

> "Social evolution is the resultant of the interaction of two wholly distinct factors: the individual... bearing all the power of initiative and origination in his hands; and, second, the social environment, with its power of adopting or rejecting both him and his gifts. Both factors are essential to change. The community stagnates without the impulse of the individual. The impulse dies away without the sympathy of the community."
> -William James (1842-1910)

We're all connected. For society to evolve, its individuals must evolve. In order for individuals to evolve, we must be supported by society. Our growth goes hand in hand. When you look at how certain trends arise, you can find some examples of just how this works. Yoga has been around for centuries, but it is just recently here in the west that it has become something of a phenomenon! It seems like there are yoga studios popping up everywhere. And how cool is that? Maybe as more individuals become vegetarians, we will have more vegetarian restaurants to choose from. The relationship between the individual and society can create remarkable evolution! *-Lissa Coffey*

> "A vital force is active in every individual and leads it towards its own evolution."
> -Maria Montessori (1870-1952)

If our purpose is to learn and to grow, then evolution is inevitable. We are drawn towards that which challenges us, which strengthens us, which supports us in our endeavors – all of life is evolution. We can't turn it off. We can accelerate the process, by putting ourselves out there and experiencing what life has to offer and by making things happen for ourselves. And we can embrace the process, and enjoy the process, because we know that it just gets more wonderful and exciting and fulfilling as we go along. *-Lissa Coffey*

> "The whole process of evolution, for the Spirit, is an awakening to the truths, and the means of implementation of those truths, that are eternally present in itself."
> -N. Sri Ram (1889- ?)

Evolution in this case means growth, and especially spiritual growth. In the definition above, evolution seems to be a natural process – an "awakening." Whether we wake up gradually, with the light of dawn, or suddenly, with some kind of an alarm, we do wake up. It is in the awakened state that we are productive. And in the spiritually awakened state the infinite possibilities of the universe are as much a reality to us as the start of a new day. *-Lissa Coffey*

Example

"Human models are more vivid and more persuasive than explicit moral commands."
-Daniel J. Boorstin

An example is an illustration – it's the action in the saying that "actions speak louder than words." Our behavior, whether we're aware of it or not, sets an example to whomever is watching. We're sending subtle messages all the time. Are we paying attention to our own behavior and what it is "saying" about us? *-Lissa Coffey*

"Nothing is so contagious as example, and our every really good or bad action inspires a similar one."
-La Rouchefoucauld (1613-1790)

Think of the possibilities. Doing anonymous good deeds suddenly becomes "cool." Volunteering becomes the favorite national past-time. We smile at strangers, and strangers become friends. It's totally possible. And we can start with our own example, right here and now. *-Lissa Coffey*

"Be noble! And the nobleness that lies In other men, sleeping, but never dead, Will rise in majesty to meet thine own."
-James Russell Lowell (1819-1891)

We each have this light within us. Let it shine! When one light shines it is enough to illuminate the darkness. It gives a reminder, an example to other lights of what the brightness looks like. And soon a glow is cast which can light up the world! *-Lissa Coffey*

"Example, the surest method of instruction."
-Pliny the Younger (A.D. 62? - 113?)

Can you learn to ride a bike by reading a book? You have to actually get on the bike to figure it out. And it helps to have a friend there to show you how to do it. It's the same thing with parenting. We can tell kids to be kind, but it makes a greater impression on them if they observe and experience our kindness themselves. And we can encourage them when we see them following our example. *-Lissa Coffey*

**"You can preach a better sermon with your life than
with your lips."**
-Oliver Goldsmith (1728-1774)

There's another saying that talk is cheap. Sure, it's easy to say something, but it takes time and effort to take action on it. Live life by example. We can't just say that we're "into the environment" and then go around driving SUVs and eating out of non-recyclable Styrofoam. Our actions give our words their meaning, and make them carry more weight. *-Lissa Coffey*

Excellence

**"The secret of joy in work is contained in one word –
excellence. To know how to do something well is to enjoy it."**
-Pearl S. Buck (1964)

When we enjoy doing something, we put our heart into it, and it shows. What we enjoy doing, we do well, we can't help it. And by the same token, what we do well brings us joy! We are rewarded for a job well done by feeling good about it. *-Lissa Coffey*

**"Excellence is not an act but a habit. The things you
do the most are the things you will do best."**
-Marva Collins (1987)

It would be easy if talent was all it took for us to achieve excellence. But it doesn't work that way. On "American Idol" there are many singers with talent. But the ones who have the most experience really stand out. The experience of singing for people over and over again hones their skills, and when the competition day comes, their excellence shows. We even see how week after week, each of the singers seems to get better. They're in an environment where they are focusing their energies and spending their time to cultivating excellence. *-Lissa Coffey*

**"When we do the best that we can, we never know what
miracle is wrought in our life, or in the life of another."**
-Helen Keller (1914)

Excellence is difficult to measure. In the Olympics there is a judging system of points and scores to compare the athlete's performances. But when it comes to our day to day lives, excellence for each one of us is doing the best that we can do. We know when we're slacking off. We know when we can do better. We're the only ones who can make that judgment accurately. And when we do strive for excellence, when we put ourselves out there and really give it our all, we know it, we can feel it. *-Lissa Coffey*

> **"If people know how hard I have had to work to gain
> my mastery, it wouldn't seem so wonderful."**
> -Michelangelo (1475-1564)

Can you imagine, back in Michelangelo's time, the artists who felt jealous of his talent? Some of them may have though: "He's so good, I'll never be as good, I might as well not even try." But here Michelangelo is basically saying that anyone can have that excellence. He's saying that he worked hard to gain mastery of his art. How many of us are willing to put in the work necessary to achieve the excellence that we so desire? -*Lissa Coffey*

> **"If a man write a better book, preach a better sermon,
> or make a better mousetrap than his neighbor, though
> he build his house in the woods, the world will make a
> beaten path to his door."**
> -Ralph Waldo Emerson (1803-1882)

Excellence is noticed in this society. Excellence is honored. It doesn't matter if it comes with an award, or a paycheck, or the appreciation of others, or even just our own peace of mind knowing that we have done something good – excellence is its own reward. -*Lissa Coffey*

Expectations

> **"We expect more of ourselves than we have any right to."**
> -Oliver Wendell Holmes, Jr.

When I was 16, I participated in what was to be the first of many workshops I've been going to in the area of personal growth and self-improvement. I learned many things that weekend, but the one thing that has stuck with me, and has proven to be true over all these years is this: "Unfulfilled expectations cause upset." Think about it. Years later I learned from "A Course in Miracles" that "I am never upset for the reasons I think." What causes our "upsets" is not that things go wrong, but that we expected them to go a certain way and our expectations went unfulfilled. -*Lissa Coffey*

> **"I can't write a book commensurate with Shakespeare,
> but I can write a book by me."**
> -Sir Walter Raleigh

The one expectation we can have for ourselves is to do the best that we can. We can't expect to always be the best (and who is to judge just what qualifies as best anyway?) but we can always be original, because that's exactly what we are. No matter what we do, when we put ourselves into it, we are doing well. -*Lissa Coffey*

> **"We would have to settle for the elegant goal of
> becoming ourselves."**
> -William Styron

We set goals. We reach goals. We set new goals. And what happens? All along the way we are learning and growing. Eventually we find that the goals are somewhat arbitrary. There may be different ways for each of us to "get there" but we arrive at the same place: discovering the beauty, the wisdom, the joy within us – the beauty, the wisdom, the joy that is us. -*Lissa Coffey*

"I long to accomplish a great and noble task, but it is my chief duty to accomplish small tasks as if they were great and noble."
-Helen Keller

There's a bumper sticker that reads: "Think Globally, Act Locally." This can be applied to every area of our lives. If we expect clean air, and a clean environment, then it is up to us to do what we can, right where we are, to make this happen. If we expect peace on earth, then we are kind to people we meet, and do what we can to help others. Every action we take, no matter how big or small we perceive it to be, has an effect on the world as a whole. -*Lissa Coffey*

"To wish to act like angels while we are still in this world is nothing but folly."
-Saint Teresa of Avila

We put such expectations on ourselves! And look at the expectations we put on our children, our parents, and all the people in our lives. We are human. We are here to learn. We are going to make mistakes, it's all part of the process. When we relax our expectations and just go with the flow – approach our challenges as lessons rather than failures – then our experiences in life are more meaningful. -*Lissa Coffey*

"Because you're not what I would have you to be, I blind myself to who, in truth, you are."
-Madeline L'Engle

When I was 16 I took my first "self-help" class, and I still remember the lessons I learned there. One of the big ones was: "Unfulfilled expectations cause upset." Expectations give us some pre-set notion of what we think "should" be. When we come in to a situation without expectations, we're much more open and willing to accept, and even enjoy, what is taking place. -*Lissa Coffey*

"Expecting the world to treat you fairly because you are a good person is a little like expecting the bull not to attack you because you're a vegetarian."
-Dennis Wholey

Remember Doris Day singing: "Que sera sera, whatever will be, will be"? That's a song about no expectations. No expectations means no attachment to outcome, and that means that we can be content no matter what happens because we know that there's a reason, or a higher purpose, behind divine organization and we can accept that. -*Lissa Coffey*